AF840985

Melissa Stock is a barrister practising in data, privacy and information law. She advises and represents individuals, company, and non-governmental organisations in all areas of privacy and data protection. Melissa also advises on data governance issues and the use and ownership of data more broadly in a policy and international context. She regularly publishes articles on these areas of law and has a blog dedicated to topics relevant to privacy (www.privacylawbarrister.com) and also hosts the podcast 'the Data Optimist'.

Biometric Data and New Technologies – The Law and Practical Issues

on Technologies Such as CCTV, Facial Recognition and Drones

Biometric Data and New Technologies – The Law and Practical Issues

on Technologies Such as CCTV, Facial Recognition and Drones

Melissa Stock

Barrister, Lincoln's Inn

MA BA(Hons)

Law Brief Publishing

Published 2022 by Law Brief Publishing, an imprint of Law Brief Publishing Ltd
30 The Parks
Minehead
Somerset
TA24 8BT

www.lawbriefpublishing.com

Paperback: 978-1-913715-93-9

To my family, for all their love and patience.

PREFACE

This book is for legal practitioners, privacy professionals, data protection officers, organisations that are developing or using new technologies and biometric data, and anyone who is interested in the law that governs the control of personal information, in particular in relation to technology. The key areas of data protection and privacy law that are relevant to new technologies are explored, and the most recent cases and investigations in relation to CCTV, facial recognition, drones and emotion analysis are reviewed.

The stated law in this book is up to date as at 10 February 2022. Data protection law is an evolving area of law and in particular in the context of new technologies and biometric data, which are also being developed at a rapid pace. As such, the law as it stands is likely to change. This book is not intended to be a substitute for legal advice.

Melissa Stock
February 2022

CONTENTS

Chapter One	Introduction	1
Chapter Two	Privacy and Data Protection	3
Chapter Three	The General Data Protection Regulation and the Data Protection Act 2018	11
Chapter Four	Biometric Data	27
Chapter Five	CCTV	47
Chapter Six	Drones	69
Chapter Seven	Facial Recognition	79
Chapter Eight	Emotion Recognition	99
Chapter Nine	Artificial Intelligence	107
Chapter Ten	Conclusion	121

CHAPTER ONE

INTRODUCTION

Biometric data are data that identify a person through measurements and calculations that relate to human characteristics. Biometric data are increasingly being used in both the public and private sectors, most commonly as a form of authentication, but novel technologies involving the processing of biometric data are emerging. The advances in artificial intelligence and the use of so-called 'big data' will also have significant implications for individuals and their personal data.

The Data Protection Directive 95/46/EC[1] was introduced in 1995 and implemented in the United Kingdom ('UK') by the Data Protection Act 1998 ('DPA 1998'). Its introduction was a big step forward in data protection and was the result of a move towards harmonising the approach of the European Union's Member States to protecting personal data. This was becoming more relevant with the increasing use of technology. But we could not predict just quite how significant technological advances would be, or how fundamental the use of personal data would become in our societies. To put this into perspective: at the time the Directive was enacted Google, Facebook, Twitter, YouTube and iPhones did not exist. The General Data Protection Regulation (EU) 2016/679 ('the GDPR') was introduced in 2016[2] to bring data protection legislation up to date with the extraordinary and unanticipated advances in technology and the way that society now uses personal data.

The GDPR, while 'technology neutral', prohibits the processing of biometric data unless certain additional obligations are met. This is still a developing area of law and the application of the recent data protection

---

1 'Of the European Parliament and of the Council of 24 October 1995 on the protection of individuals with regard to the processing of personal data and on the free movement of such data'.

2 The GDPR was implemented in 2018.

rules to the use of biometric data in various novel technologies is uncertain. Nevertheless, this book aims to explain how data protection and privacy law applies to various new technologies, reviews the recent or relevant case law, and provides available best practice advice and guidance for those organisations that are using, applying, or developing these technologies.

Chapter II of this book explains the interrelationship between data protection law and privacy law. Chapter III outlines the fundamental data protection concepts in the GDPR (the 'UK GDPR' in the UK) and explains who it applies to, the obligations that it imposes, the rights it provides, and the remedies that can be sought when data protection law is contravened. Chapter IV sets out the specific rules that apply to the use of biometric data and includes an examination of 'profiling' of individuals.

Thereafter, this book discusses some particular new technologies. Chapter V identifies the law that is applicable to closed-circuit television ('CCTV') and reviews the relevant case law and regulatory investigations. In 2020, there was a significant case in the Court of Appeal in relation to facial recognition technology. Chapter VI examines this case in detail and provides an overview of the steps that will be expected of organisations that are creating or using facial recognition technology. Chapter VII examines the use of drones. Chapter VIII examines a technology that is in its nascent stages of development, but which will be relevant in the next decade: emotion recognition. Chapter IX is dedicated to a discussion of artificial intelligence and the challenges in its use in relation to data protection.

CHAPTER TWO

PRIVACY AND DATA PROTECTION

There is an overlapping relationship between data protection and privacy law, although the interrelationship between the two can often be complex. As an area of law which is still developing it is not always clear how the relationship will change over time. Added to this complexity is Brexit, which has removed the UK from the European Union ('EU') while retaining the majority of the legislation that was enacted while still part of Europe.

The 'right to privacy' and the 'right to data protection' have been given equal importance by the Charter of Fundamental Rights of the EU ('the Charter') and yet the relationship between privacy and data protection is not straightforward. Prior to the incorporation of the Charter into EU law as part of the Treaty of Lisbon in 2009, the Court of Justice of the European Union ('CJEU') cited the provisions of the European Convention on Human Rights ('the Convention') when interpreting the Data Protection Directive in relation to fundamental rights.

Article 7 of the Charter, 'Respect for Private and Family Life', provides that '*everyone has the right to respect for his or her private and family life, home and communications*'. The wording reflects, in part, Article 8 of the Convention, which is as follows:

> '1. *Everyone has the right to respect for his private and family life, his home and his correspondence.*
>
> 2. *There shall be no interference by a public authority with the exercise of this right except such as is in accordance with the law and is necessary in a democratic society in the interests of national security, public safety or the economic well-being of the country, for the prevention of disorder or crime, for the protection of health or morals, or for the protection of the rights and freedoms of others.*'

The close connection between Article 7 of the Charter and Article 8 of the Convention was highlighted by the CJEU in *Volker und Markus Schecke GbR and Hartmut Eifert v Land Hessen.*[3]However, it is important to note that there are differences in the way that private life is interpreted by the European Court of Human Rights ('ECtHR') and the CJEU in respect to data protection, in part because of the requirement of finding 'necessity' in Article 8(2) of the Convention. The ECtHR has also held that data protection is capable of engaging both Article 8 of the Convention and Article 10 of the Convention ('the right to freedom of expression'),[4] while Article 7 and 8 in the Charter are distinct rights.

Article 8 of the Charter, 'Protection of Personal Data', provides as follows:

> *'8(1): Everyone has the right to the protection of personal data concerning him or her.*
>
> *8(2): Such data must be processed fairly for specified purposes and on the basis of the consent of the person concerned or some other legitimate basis laid down by law. Everyone has the right of access to data which has been collected concerning him or her, and the right to have it rectified.*
>
> *8(3): Compliance with these rules shall be subject to control by an independent authority.'*

There is a growing body of case law in the CJEU referring to the right to data protection provided by Article 8 of the Charter. Examples include:

- Fingerprints and passports – *Michael Schwarz v Stadt Bochum, Case C-291/12, 17 October 2013.*[5]

[3] CJEU *Cases C-468/10 and C-469/10,* 9 November 2010, ECLI:EU:C:2010:662, at paragraph 47.

[4] See the cases *McMichael v UK (1995) 20 EHRR 205* and *Társaság a Szabadságjogokért v. Hungary*, application no. 37374/05, 14 April 2009.

[5] ECLI:EU:C:2013:670.

- Electronic communications – *Digital Rights Ireland Ltd v Ireland, Case C-293/12 and Case C-594-12, 8 April 2014.*[6]

- Social media data – *Maximillian Schrems v Data Protection Commissioner Case C-362/14, 6 October 2015*[7]*; Data Protection Commissioner v Facebook Ireland Limited, Maximillian Schrems Case C-311/18, 16 July 2020.*[8]

- Door-to-door data collection – *Tietosuojavaltuutettu v Jehovan todistajat – uskonnollinen yhdyskunta, Case C-25/17, 10 July 2018.*[9]

- 'YouTube' postings – *Sergejs Buivids v. Datu valsts inspekcija, Case C-345/17, 14 February 2019.*[10]

- Directories – *Deutsche Telekom AG v Bundesrepublik Deutschland, Case C-543/09, 5 May 2011.*[11]

Despite the fact that privacy and data protection are defined as two separate rights in the Charter, the jurisprudence of Europe's highest courts has considered there to be an interrelationship between privacy and data protection. The CJEU has interpreted the scope of private life as including the protection of personal data: *'it must be considered that the right to respect for private life with regard to the processing of personal data, recognised by Articles 7 and 8 of the Charter, concerns any information relating to an identified or identifiable individual and the limitations which*

[6] ECLI:EU:C:2014:238.

[7] ECLI:EU:C:2015:650.

[8] ECLI:EU:C:2020:559.

[9] ECLI:EU:C:2018:551.

[10] ECLI:EU:C:2019:122.

[11] ECLI:EU:C:2011:279.

may lawfully be imposed on the right to the protection of personal data correspond to those tolerated in relation to Article 8 of the Convention'.[12]

The ECtHR has, in a number of cases, similarly found a connection between personal data and the right to private life, finding that the storing of personal data falls within the ambit of Article 8 of the Convention.[13] A broad range of data has been considered by the ECtHR in the context of private life, including: telecommunications data,[14] personal information in public files,[15] analysis of internet and telephone usage,[16] DNA and fingerprint records,[17] personal information placed in an online advertisement,[18] and a record of a spent conviction.[19]

However, it is unclear how privacy as defined by the Convention will influence the interpretation of the fundamental rights and freedoms referred to in the GDPR. The GDPR has expanded the approach to data protection so that all rights and freedoms that are affected by data processing are now relevant. It incorporates <u>all</u> fundamental rights and freedoms recognised in the Charter:

> *'This Regulation respects all fundamental rights and observes the freedoms and principles recognised in the Charter as enshrined in the Treaties, in particular the respect for private and family life, home and communications, the protection of personal data, freedom of thought, conscience and religion, freedom of expression and information, freedom to conduct a business, the*

---

[12] *Volker und Markus Schecke GbR*, ibid., paragraph 52.

[13] *Leander v Sweden, 26 March 1987, Series A no. 116; Amann v Switzerland, Application No. 27798/95, 16 February 2000; Rotaru v Romania, Application No. 28341/95, 4 May 2000; Segerstedt- Wiberg and Others v. Sweden, no. 62332/00, 6 June 2006.*

[14] *Liberty & Others v United Kingdom, Application No. 58234/00, 1 July 2008.*

[15] *Volker und Markus Schecke GbR*, ibid.

[16] *Copland v. United Kingdom, Application No. 62617/00, 3 April 2007.*

[17] *S&Marper v UK, Application Nos. 30562/04 and 30566/04, 4 December 2008.*

[18] *K.U. v. Finland, Application No. 2872/02, 2 December 2.*

[19] *MM v U.K. Application No. 24029/07 (13 November 2012).*

> *right to an effective remedy and to a fair trial, and cultural, religious and linguistic diversity'.*[20]

These fundamental rights and freedoms go beyond that of privacy and data protection, such that it must therefore be borne in mind that the GDPR can be applied by individuals to safeguard a variety of interests, albeit that the starting point will need to be some sort of interference with their personal data. Accordingly, it will be important to be aware of the jurisprudence in relation to other rights, which have been affected by the processing of personal data, and that has caused undesirable outcomes or differential treatment. This may also include the impact on a fundamental right as a result of a data subject enforcing a data protection right. In *Volker und Markus Scheke GbR*, the court described the right to data protection under the Charter as one which is not absolute, and which must be considered in relation to its function in society.[21]

Examples:

- Discrimination – *Huber v Germany, Case C-524/06, 16 December 2008.*[22]
- The right to an effective remedy – *Data Protection Commissioner v Facebook Ireland Limited, Maximillian Schrems Case C-311/18, 16 July 2020.*[23]
- Freedom of expression – *Bodil Lindqvist v Åklagarkammaren i Jönköping, Case C-101/01, 6 November 2003.*[24]

---

20 Recital 4 of the GDPR. 'Fundamental rights and freedoms' are referred to throughout the GDPR, see recitals 2, 10, 16, 47, 51, 69, and 113.

21 *Volker und Markus Schecke GbR*, ibid., paragraph 48.

22 ECLI:EU:C:2008:724.

23 Ibid., footnote 6.

24 ECLI:EU:C:2003:596.

- Protection of property – *Promusicae v Telefónica de España SAU, Case C-275/06, 29 January 2008,*[25]*Scarlet Extended SA v Société belge des auteurs, compositeurs et éditeurs SCRL (SABAM), Case C-70/10, 24 November 2011.*[26]

- Access to documents – *Egan & Hackett v European Parliament, Case T-190/10, 28 March 2012.*[27]

Privacy law claims in the UK are usually brought under the cause of action of 'misuse of private information'. This is a relatively new tort that emerged in the common law to give effect to Article 8 of the Convention so that an individual could protect their right to privacy where there was no pre-existing relationship of confidence. The tort was first realised in the case of *Campbell v Mirror Group Newspapers Ltd [2004] UKHL*, which extended the law of confidence to protect individuals from unlawful disclosure of information in which they have 'a reasonable expectation of privacy'.

There is a two-stage test to establish the cause of action. The first stage is to establish whether the claimant has a reasonable expectation of privacy in relation to the information that forms the subject of the claim. This involves an objective assessment of the circumstances in the case, including: the attributes of the claimant, the nature and purpose of the use of the information, the effect the use has on the claimant, and the circumstances in which the information came into the possession of the discloser (see *Murray v Express Newspapers Plc [2008] Civ 466*). There is no presumption that a reasonable expectation of privacy is lost if the information is in the public domain, but the degree to which it undermines the right must be assessed by the court.

If the first stage is established, then the second stage is to determine whether in all the circumstances, the privacy rights of the claimant is

---

[25] ECLI:EU:C:2008:54.

[26] ECLI:EU:C:2011:771.

[27] ECLI:EU:T:2012:165.

outweighed by the other party's countervailing interests. In most cases to date, this has been the right to freedom of expression, although there may be other legitimate interests of the discloser that could be considered. Misuse of private information is a more attractive claim to pursue by claimants because it has received much higher awards in damages than in data protection claims.[28]

[28] The case of Gulati v MGN Ltd [2015] EWHC 1482 (Ch) established the methodology for awards in misuse of private information claims.

CHAPTER THREE

THE GENERAL DATA PROTECTION REGULATION AND THE DATA PROTECTION ACT 2018

The GDPR came into effect on 25 May 2018, replacing the Data Protection Directive 95/46/EC. As a regulation, it had direct effect in the UK when the UK was part of the EU. This meant that it did not need to be implemented by national legislation, although the GDPR permitted Member States to enact legislation to make provisions for derogations and exemptions. The UK enacted the Data Protection Act 2018 ('DPA 2018'), which replaced the DPA 1998.[29]

In the process of leaving the EU,[30] the European Union (Withdrawal) Act 2018 was enacted and saves EU law as it applied to the UK at the end of the transition period.[31] This is known as 'retained EU law' and was introduced so that the large proportion of UK law that is based on EU law did not need to be replaced immediately. The Data Protection, Privacy and Electronic Communications (Amendments etc)(EU Exit) Regulations 2020 ('Exit Regulations') amend the GDPR and the DPA 2018 to allow them to operate in the UK now that we are no longer part of the EU.

The Exit Regulations create the 'UK GDPR', which operates as standalone legislation. The Exit Regulations make hundreds of changes to the GDPR and to the DPA 2018. These changes have been consolidated into two Keeling Schedules, and these should be referred to

---

[29] The Data Protection Act 1998 implemented the Data Protection Directive (95/46/EC).

[30] Often referred to as 'Brexit'.

[31] The Transition period took place between 31 January 2020 and 31 December 2020.

until a consolidating act is introduced in the UK.[32] The UK GDPR is predominantly unchanged from the GDPR that applied up until the end of the withdrawal period but will at some point be replaced.[33]

The structure of the DPA 2018 is unlike the UK GDPR. It replicates some of the UK GDPR but applies certain adaptations, restrictions and exemptions. The DPA 2018 has seven parts and data processing is separated into sectors. Parts 3 and 4 of the DPA 2018 cover law enforcement and intelligences services respectively. Part 2 of the DPA 2018 deals with 'general processing', that is, all other sectors, subject to the modifications outlined in Chapter 3 of Part 2 of the DPA 2018.

Before looking at how specific technologies and biometric data are dealt with it is important to understand some fundamental concepts in data protection law.

Fundamental Concepts

What information does data protection law apply to?

The UK GDPR and DPA 2018 apply to **personal data.** Personal data is given a broad definition in the UK GDPR. It is defined in Article 4(1):

> *'Personal data' means any information relating to an identified or identifiable natural person 'data subject'; an identifiable person is one who can be identified, directly or indirectly, in particular by reference to an identifier such as a name, an identification number, location data, an online identifier or to one or more factors specific to the physical, physiological, genetic,*

---

[32] Available here: https://assets.publishing.service.gov.uk/government/uploads/system/uploads/attachment_data/file/685632/2018-03-05_Keeling_Schedule.pdf

[33] See UK Department for Digital, Culture, Media & Sport press release dated 26 August 2021: https://www.gov.uk/government/news/uk-unveils-post-brexit-global-data-plans-to-boost-growth-increase-trade-and-improve-healthcare

mental, economic, cultural or social identity of that natural person'.

'Any information' means that any format or type of information – video, written records, audio files, photographs etc. – is subject to the GDPR. The information does not need to relate to an individual in their private or family life as defined by Article 8 of the Convention; the approach is 'agnostic' in this regard.

Who does data protection law protect?

The **data subject** is defined as an identified, or identifiable natural person and has a number of rights in relation to the processing of his or her personal data.[34] A data subject must be a 'natural person' and not a 'legal person'. Although there could arguably be an exception for sole traders, or individuals whose persona cannot be separated from their trading business or their organisation.[35]

The personal data may not alone identify the person but does so when combined with other information. There may be more than one data subject associated with the personal data.[36] For example, a postal address may reveal the identity of more than one person who lives in the household at that address.

The data subject has a number of **data rights**. These are:

- The right to be informed (UK GDPR Article 14)
- The right of access (UK GDPR Article 15)
- The right of rectification (UK GDPR Article 16)

---

[34] UK GDPR Article 4(1), and Part 1 section 3(5) DPA 2018.

[35] *Volker und Markus Schecke GbR and Hartmut Eifert v Land Hessen.*

[36] *Peter Nowak v Data Protection Commissioner Case C-434/16,* 20 December 2017, ECLI:EU:C:2017:994.

- The right to erasure (UK GDPR Article 17)
- The right to object (UK GDPR Article 21)
- The right to data portability (UK GDPR Article 20)
- Rights in relation to automated decision making and profiling (UK GDPR Article 22)
- The right to restrict processing (UK GDPR Article 18)

Who can the rights be enforced against?

'**Processing**' is defined in UK GDPR Article 4(2) and Part 1 section 3(4) DPA 2018 and means anything done to data including collecting, recording, organising, storing, adapting and deleting. The processing must be wholly or partly automated. If it is not automated, it does not fall within the scope of the UK GDPR and the DPA 2018 unless the personal data forms, or is intended to form, part of a filing system.[37] For example, if information, or data, is communicated over the telephone, but is not recorded, it does not fall within the scope of the data protection rules.[38]

Organisations and individuals processing personal data for professional, commercial, charitable, non-profit or public sector reasons, will come under the ambit of the UK GDPR and are defined as either '**controllers**' or '**processors**'. A controller is defined in UK GDPR Article 4(7) and Part 2 section 6(1) DPA 2018 (for general processing) as a *'person or body which, alone or jointly with others, determines the purposes and means of the processing of personal data'.* Who is the controller is a question of fact. There may be situations where two organisations process the personal data and become 'joint controllers'.[39]

---

[37] Article 2(1) UK GDPR and Part 2, Chapter 1, section 4(2) DPA 2018.

[38] See *Scott v LGBT Foundation Ltd [2020] EWHC 483 (QB).*

[39] UK GDPR Article 26 and Part 1, section 5(1) DPA 2018.

A processor is defined in UK GDPR Article 4(8) and section 5(1) DPA 2018 (general processing) as a *'natural or legal person, public authority, agency or other body which processes personal data on behalf of the controller'*. Processors may also be controllers in respect to certain actions taken on the same set of personal data or different sets of personal data. There must be a written contract between the controller and processor.[40]

Those processing personal data in a 'purely personal or household activity' will generally not be subject to the UK GDPR.[41]

Where does it apply?

According to Article 3 of the UK GDPR, it applies in the following situations:

(1) When an organisation is 'established' in the UK (regardless of whether or not the processing takes place in the UK);

(2) Where there is 'monitoring' of UK data subjects, or the offering of goods or services to UK data subjects, even if the controller or processor is not in the UK; and

(3) Where the organisation is not in the UK, but domestic law applies by virtue of public international law.

Knowing when the UK GDPR applies is not always a straightforward analysis. It is important to understand that its applicability is not confined to the nationality of the data subjects, the location where the controllers or processors are legally incorporated, or where the processing takes place. This territorial scope is identical in the DPA 2018.

---

[40] UK GDPR Article 28(3).

[41] UK GDPR Article 2(c).

What obligations do controllers and processors have?

<u>The Data Protection Principles</u>

When processing personal data, controllers and processors must adhere to the six principles in Article 5 of the UK GDPR:[42]

(1) Lawfulness, fairness and transparency;

(2) Purpose limitation;

(3) Data minimisation;

(4) Accuracy;

(5) Storage limitation; and

(6) Integrity and confidentiality.

To comply with the principles, there are a number of obligations that are set out in Chapters II, III, IV and V of the UK GDPR.

<u>A Lawful Basis</u>

To comply with the first data protection principle, the controller and/or processor must have a lawful basis under UK GDPR Article 6(1). These are as follows:

- **Consent** (Article 6(1)(a))
- The performance of a **contract**, or steps taken prior to entering the contract at the request of the data subject (Article 6(1)(b))
- To comply with a **legal obligation** (Article 6(1)(c))

[42] Part 1 section 2 and Part 2 section 4 of DPA 2018.

- To protect the **vital interests** of a data subject or natural person (Article 6(1)(d))

- For the performance of a task carried out in the **public interest** or under **official authority** (Article 6(1)(e))

- For the purposes of **legitimate interests** pursued by the controller or third party, except where such interests are overridden by the interests or fundamental rights and freedoms of the data subject which require protection of personal data, in particular where the data subject is a child (Article 6(1)(f))

There are certain 'rules' to the application of the lawful basis. First, the lawful grounds and purpose for each processing operation must be determined at the outset.[43] Second, it is not possible for a controller to 'switch' a legal basis for processing at a later date. That is, a controller cannot rely on consent when it collects the data for processing for a particular purpose, and then switch to legitimate interest for another purpose.

Third, there cannot be more than one legal basis that applies to the same processing action, although there can be more than one legal basis that applies to the personal data where there are multiple processing actions. For example, an online retailer processes a person's name to send them an item (contract), and also processes the person's name when keeping a record of the transaction (legitimate interest).

The ICO recommends that controllers approach the legal basis of legitimate interests as a three-stage test.[44] The controller must show:

(1) That there is a legitimate interest for the processing (the 'purpose' test)

---

[43] Ibid., paragraphs 116 to 120.

[44] ICO guidance on legitimate interests: https://ico.org.uk/for-organisations/guide-to-data-protection/guide-to-the-general-data-protection-regulation-gdpr/legitimate-interests/what-is-the-legitimate-interests-basis/#three_part_test

(2) The processing is necessary for that purpose (the 'necessity' test)

(3) The legitimate interest is not overridden by the individual's interests, rights or freedoms (the 'balancing' test).

Law Enforcement Processing

Part 3, Chapter 2 of the DPA 2018 sets out the data protection obligations for the processing of personal data for law enforcement purposes and implements the Law Enforcement Directive 2016/680. Section 35 DPA 2018 outlines the data protection principles that apply and include the concept that the processing must be:

- Lawful and fair (section 35(1));
- Specified, explicit and legitimate (section 36(1)(a));
- In a manner compatible with the purpose for which it was collected (section 36(1)(b));
- Adequate, relevant and not excessive (section 37);
- Processing data that is accurate and up to date, and rectified or deleted if not (section 38(1));
- Using personal data that is not kept for longer than is necessary for the purpose of the processing (section 39); and
- Applying appropriate technical and organisational measures to ensure the security of the personal data (section 40).

Anonymisation/Pseudonymisation

Where an organisation processes personal data that on its own does not identify a person (referred to as 'pseudonymised' data) but that when combined with other information it becomes possible to identify a person, then the pseudonymised data falls within the UK GDPR rules. It does not matter if the 'other information' is held by a different controller, organisation, or is available elsewhere.[45] Recital 26 of the GDPR gives some assistance in the question of whether or not a person is 'identifiable' from the pseudonymised data stating: '*account should be taken of all the means reasonably likely to be used, such as singling out, either by the controller or by another person to identify the natural person directly or indirectly*'.

Data that that has been anonymised is no longer considered to be personal data under the UK GDPR. There is often confusion between pseudonymised (or de-identified data) and anonymised data. Sometimes organisations refer to personal data being anonymised when in fact they have been pseudonymised.[46]

Recital 30 of the GDPR explains that online identifiers are those identifiers provided by '*devices, applications, tools and protocols*', from which a person may be identified by combining those identifiers with unique identifiers and information received by servers. These identifiers, combined with other information, may be used to create profiles of persons, and identify them.

<u>The Special Categories</u>

There are also what are known as 'special categories' of personal data, over which organisations have additional responsibilities given their sensitive nature. The special categories are listed in UK GDPR Article 9(1) and are personal data relating to:

- Racial or ethnic origin
- Political opinion
- Religious or philosophical beliefs

---

[45] See *Patrick Breyer v Bundesrepublik Deutschland CJEU Case C-582/14,* 19 October 2016, ECLI: EU:C:2016:779.

[46] For the definition in the UK GDPR, see Article 4(5).

- Trade union membership
- Health
- Sex life or sexual orientation
- Genetic data
- Biometric data (processed to uniquely identify a person)

Processing by an organisation of these categories of personal data is prohibited, unless one of the lawful processing conditions under UK GDPR Article 9(2) or Schedule 1 to the DPA 2018 applies. Organisations must still comply with all other UK GDPR principles, including having a lawful basis in Article 6(1).[47]

Informing the Data Subject

The first data protection principle requires that organisations are transparent in the way that they use personal data. A data subject has the right to receive information from an organisation to understand how his or her data is being used. For example, the organisation must inform the data subject what purposes it is pursuing, what lawful basis is relied upon, if the data are given to other parties and the rights that are available to the data subject. The 'information requirements' can be found in UK GDPR Article 13 and Article 14. Article 13 is relevant where the personal data are collected directly from the data subject. Article 14 applies where the personal data have not been obtained from the data subject, but from some other source.

Remedies

Under UK GDPR Article 82 and section 168 of the DPA 2018 it is possible to claim damages for compensation from the controller or processor of the personal data for material or non-material damage caused by an infringement. Causation principles apply and the claimant will

[47] Part 2 sections 10(1) to (3) DPA 2018.

need to prove that the damage was '*caused by processing which infringes this Regulation*'.[48] The claim may be brought against a controller who is '*involved in processing*', and/or a processor who has '*not complied with obligations of this Regulation specifically directed to processors or where it has acted outside or contrary to lawful instructions of the controller*'.[49]

Any contracts that exist between the controller, processor and (where relevant) sub-processors, will not affect the right of the claimant to bring legal action against the parties, even if the contracts apportion liability between them. UK GDPR Article 82(5) entitles controllers and processors to seek compensation for their corresponding responsibility for the damage from other controllers and processors.

There is a defence under UK GDPR Article 82(3), which provides an exemption from liability if a controller or processor '*proves that it is not in any way responsible for the event giving rise to the damage*'.

A controller or processor may also be vicariously liable for the actions of another that lead to an infringement of the UK GDPR. However, in the case of *WM Morrison Supermarket Plc v Various Claimants [2020] UKSC12*, the Supreme Court overturned the decision of the Court of Appeal. The Supreme Court decided, unanimously, that WM Morrison was not liable for the data breaches facilitated by one of its employees, who had acted illegally to steal data from the company. It was affirmed that the approach taken in *Mohamud v William Morrison Supermarket Plc [2016] UKSC11* was correct. The court stated that the decision did not depart from the principle that vicarious liability can be established where the unauthorized acts of an employee are so closely connected with acts which the employer has authorized, that they can be regarded as being within the scope of employment. While on this occasion the facts did not support the 'close connection' test, vicarious liability may be established in other scenarios.

A claimant may seek compensation for material or non-material damage i.e. financial loss or distress. Damages are awarded on tortious principles,

48 UK GDPR Article 82(2).

49 Ibid.

such that they aim to put the claimant in the position which she or he would have been had the infringement not occurred. GDPR recital 75 describes the possible impact on data subjects, which includes:

- Discrimination;
- Identity theft and fraud;
- Financial loss;
- Damage to reputation;
- Loss of confidentiality of personal data protected by professional secrecy;
- Unauthorised reversal of pseudonymisation; and
- Any other significant economic or social disadvantage.

The scope of these types of effects on data subjects has not been fully explored in the UK courts. There is as yet only a small body of case law on the quantification of damages in data protection cases. The amount that a claimant may be awarded for non-material damage can be difficult to assess and will depend on the particular circumstances of the case. Most data protection cases have been brought alongside claims for defamation, misuse of private information or breach of confidence.

The Supreme Court recently considered the question of whether it is possible to claim for 'loss of control' of personal data as a consequence of an infringement of the data protection legislation. In *Lloyd v Google [2021] UKSC 50* the Supreme Court decided that it was not possible to bring a group action under the representative action procedure on the basis of a loss of control of personal data, unless there is proof that the loss of control had affected the data subject. While the court concluded that it is possible to claim for 'loss of control' of personal data, the fact of the infringement alone will not be enough to bring a claim for damages. It is also necessary to prove that the loss of control affected the data subject. The wording of UK GDPR Article 82(1) suggests that it is not possible to bring a claim where the loss of control may, or is likely to, cause damage at some point in the future.

Examples of damages awards in data protection and privacy claims

- *Gulati v MGN Ltd [2015] EWHC 1482 (Ch)* was a landmark decision on the quantum of privacy damages. Mann J made a number of awards ranging from £72,500 to £260,250, and created a 'layered' approach to quantum, that included an award for the 'loss of the right to control the use of private information'.

- *Campbell v Mirror Group Newspapers Ltd [2002] EWHC 499 (QB)*: £2,500 in damages for distress and hurt to feelings as a result of a photograph published in newspapers; £1,000 award in aggravated damages.

- *Mosley v News Group [2008] EWHC 1777 (QB)*: £60,000 for the mass publication of images revealing the claimant's sexual activities.

- *Cooper v Turrell [2011] EWHC 3269 (QB)*: £50,000 in libel, and £30,00 for misuse of private information for the disclosure of private medical information on the Internet.

- *Ali and Aslam v Channel 5 [2019] EWCA Civ 677*: £10,000 to each claimant for causing 'real distress' by broadcasting footage of them in their bedclothes in a television show.

- *ZYC v Bloomberg [2019] EWHC 970 (QB)*: the claimant was awarded £25,000 for an article that revealed he was being investigated for criminal offences.

- *Halliday v Creation Consumer Finance Ltd [2013] EWCA Civ 333*: the claimant was awarded £750 for distress as a result of an incorrect record of a debt that was shared with a credit reference agency.

The Information Commissioner's Office ('ICO')

Where a data subject is dissatisfied with a response from an organisation, or wants to challenge a refusal notice, he or she may make a request to the ICO to investigate and take regulatory action, or bring a private claim in the courts against the organisation. It is possible for the data subject to do both, and a response from the ICO is not required to initiate legal proceedings. The ICO may also decide to investigate of its own motion.

The ICO's main enforcement measures are:

- To issue an information notice requiring the controller, processor or other person to provide particular information requested;

- To issue an assessment notice against a controller or processor to enable the ICO to assess its data practices, which may involve entering premises, inspecting documents, observing processes and conducting interviews;

- To issue an enforcement notice against a controller or processor imposing certain requirements to correct the data protection failing; or

- To issue a penalty notice against a controller or processor where it has failed, or is failing, to comply with its continuing obligations or with data subjects' rights, or for failing to comply with one of the notices listed above.

The GDPR brought data protection into the spotlight, in particular, because it substantially increased the penalties that a data supervisory authority could impose. It is possible for it to fine an organisation up to 4% of its total annual worldwide turnover in the preceding financial year, or £17,500,000, whichever is the greater, for breaching data protection principles and obligations.[50] Note that whilst the ICO may pursue the

[50] UK GDPR Article 83(5) for serious infringements such as of Articles 5,6,7,9, data subject rights and transfers of personal data. UK GDPR Article 83(4) covers less

measures listed above, it will not order the organisation to pay the data subject financial compensation. Such a remedy can only be pursued in a civil claim in a court. Where an organisation disagrees with the findings of the ICO, it may appeal against the decision to the First-tier Tribunal.

The Commissioner is obliged to take steps to respond to the complaint, investigate the complaint, inform the complainant of the outcome and provide the complainant with further information to pursue the complaint.[51] It is possible to apply to the First-tier Tribunal for an order requiring the ICO to progress the complaint if no appropriate action is taken within three months,[52] however in reality, it may be more effective for the data subject to pursue a private action against the controller in the civil courts.

A claim can be brought in either the County Court or the High Court, depending on the usual principles. In general, the default position is that claims may not be brought in the High Court unless the value of the claim is more than £100,000, or there is particular complexity that warrants being heard by a specialist judge in the High Court.[53] Claimants must now follow the pre-action protocol for media and communications claims when pursuing a cause of action based on data protection if their case falls within the scope of CPR rule 53.1. The court can make compliance orders on similar terms to the ICO, that is, requiring the controller or processor to take specific steps (e.g. erase the data), and/or make an order for compensation to be paid to the claimant.

---

serious infringements, with a possible fine of up to 2% of annual worldwide turnover in the preceding financial year, or £8,700,000, whichever is the greater.

[51] UK GDPR Articles 57(1)(f) and 77(2).

[52] Section 166 DPA 2018.

[53] CPR PD7A paragraphs 2.1 and 2.4.

CHAPTER FOUR

BIOMETRIC DATA

Introduction

Biometric data are data that identify a person through measurements and calculations that relate to human characteristics. The characteristics that are included in the definition of biometric identifiers are wide and divided into the following: physiological and behavioural. Examples of physiological characteristics that can be identified are: a fingerprint or palm print, facial mapping, and iris or retina recognition. Examples of behavioural characteristics include a person's gait, voice, handwritten signature and keystroke patterns.

Data Protection Law

Biometric data are defined in the UK GDPR in Article 4(4)[54] as:

> '*personal data resulting from specific technical processing relating to the physical, physiological or behavioural characteristics of a natural person, which allow or confirm the unique identification of that natural person, such as facial images or dactyloscopic data*'.[55]

According to UK GDPR Article 9(1), the processing of biometric data for the purpose of uniquely identifying a natural person is prohibited unless one of the conditions in Article 9(2) applies. Note the specific wording of this provision means that if the processing of the biometric data is not being used to identify someone, then Article 9(1) and (2) do not apply, but it could still be considered personal data if someone is

---

[54] This definition is replicated in section 205(1) DPA 2018 except referring to 'individual' rather than 'natural person'.

[55] Dactyloscopic data means fingerprint data.

identified, or identifiable, and general data protection compliance therefore still applies.

Photographs do not automatically fall within the definition of biometric data. Recital 51states:

> *'The processing of photographs should not systematically be considered to be processing of special categories of personal data as they are covered by the definition of biometric data only when processed through a specific technical means allowing the unique identification or authentication of a natural person.'*

The conditions in Article 9(2) are as follows:

UK GDPR Reference	Description
Article 9(2)(a)	**The data subject has given explicit consent** to the processing of those personal data for one or more specified purposes, except where the law provides otherwise.
Article 9(2)(b)	**Processing is necessary** for the purposes of carrying out the obligations and exercising specific rights of the controller or of the data subject in the field of **employment** and **social security** and **social protection law** in so far as it is **authorised by law** ...providing for appropriate safeguards for the fundamental rights and the interests of the data subject.
Article 9(2)(c)	The processing of the personal data is necessary to protect the **vital interests** of the data subject or another natural person where the data subject is physically or legally incapable of giving consent.

Article 9(2)(d)	The processing is carried out by a **foundation, association** or any other **not-for-profit body** with a **political, philosophical, religious** or **trade union aim**, in the course of its legitimate activities with appropriate safeguards and on condition that the processing relates solely to members or to former members of the body, or to persons in regular contact with it, and that the personal data are not disclosed outside the body without consent of the data subjects.
Article 9(2)(e)	The processing relates to personal data which are **manifestly made public by the data subject**.
Article 9(2)(f)	The processing is necessary for the establishment, exercise or **defence of legal claims** or whenever **courts** are acting in their judicial capacity.
Article 9(2)(g)	The processing is necessary for reasons of **substantial public interest**, on the basis of law, which shall be proportionate to the aim pursued, respect the essence of the right to data protection and provide for suitable and specific measures to safeguard the fundamental rights and the interests of the data subject.
Article 9(2)(h)	The processing is necessary for the purposes of **preventative or occupational medicine**, for the assessment of the working **capacity of the employee, medical diagnosis**, the provision of **health or social care** or treatment or the **management of health or social care systems** on the basis of domestic law or pursuant to contract with a health professional and subject to the conditions and safeguards.

Article 9(2)(i)	The processing is necessary for reasons of **public interest in the area of public health**, such as protecting against serious cross-border threats to health or ensuring high standards of quality and safety of health care and of medicinal products or medical devices, on the basis of domestic law which provides for suitable and specific measures to safeguard the rights and freedoms of the data subject, in particular professional secrecy.
Article 9(2)(j)	The processing is necessary for **archiving purposes in the public interest, scientific or historical research purposes** or **statistical purposes** in accordance with Article 89(1) (as supplemented by section 19 of the 2018 Act) based on domestic law which shall be proportionate to the aim pursued, respect the essence of the right to data protection and provide for suitable and specific measures to safeguard the fundamental rights and the interests of the data subject.

This chapter considers the most relevant grounds that controllers may seek to rely on in the context of the use of biometric data and new technologies and on which further analysis may be useful.

Explicit Consent: UK GDPR Article 9(2)(a)

Explicit consent is not defined in the UK GDPR or GDPR. The conditions for consent are described in UK GDPR Article 7. The request for consent from the data subject must be clearly distinguishable from other matters, intelligible, easily accessible and put to the data subject using clear and plain language.[56] Consent must also be freely given, informed and a clear affirmative action. According to Article 7(1) the controller must be able to demonstrate that the data subject has

[56] UK GDPR Article 7(2).

consented to processing of his or her personal data. The data subject must also be able to easily withdraw consent at any time.[57]

Given that the conditions for consent under the UK GDPR/GDPR are already stringent it may appear difficult to interpret what the difference between valid consent and explicit consent would look like in practice. The ICO states that '*the key difference is likely to be that explicit consent must be expressly confirmed in words which refer to the type of special category data involved, rather than by any other positive action*'.[58] The Article 29 Working Party 'Guidelines on Consent under Regulation 2016/679' provides some useful practical guidance on how controllers can obtain explicit consent.

The GDPR permits Member States (which included the UK at the time it was introduced) to add further conditions for the use of biometric data. The UK has not as yet introduced such conditions, although processing special category data 'on the basis of law' for conditions in Article 9(2)(b), (g), (h), (i), (j) is found in the DPA 2018.

If you are an organisation that falls under the category of 'general processing' of personal data (see Chapter III), then to rely on (b), (h), (i) or (j), it is also necessary to meet the associated condition found in Schedule 1 of the DPA 2018. To rely on (g), it is also necessary to meet one of the conditions set out in Part 2 of Schedule 1 of the DPA 2018. Schedule 1 includes the additional requirement of an 'appropriate policy document' and keep records of processing in relation to special category data (see below).

The ICO makes clear that given the risks to individuals in the processing of special category data, there is more emphasis on the use of the basis of

---

[57] UK GDPR Article 7(3).

[58] See: https://ico.org.uk/for-organisations/guide-to-data-protection/key-dp-themes/guidance-for-the-use-of-personal-data-in-political-campaigning-1/special-category-data/#whatis2

explicit consent than other conditions in UK GDPR Article 9(2).[59] It is also important to note that the processing must be necessary for a specific purpose. If it is possible to achieve the same purpose in a less intrusive way, then the processing will not be considered 'necessary'. As the ICO explains: '*it is not enough to argue that processing is necessary because it is part of your particular business model, processes or procedures, or because it is standard practice. The question is whether the processing of the special category data is a targeted and proportionate way of achieving the purpose described in the condition*'.[60]

A controller that is processing biometric data to identify individuals will need to justify its decision not to seek explicit consent.

Manifestly made public: UK GDPR Article 9(2)(e)

The phrase 'manifestly made public' is not defined in the GDPR, UK GDPR or the DPA 2018. However, to rely on this ground, the ICO states that the data subject must have made his or her personal data public in an intentional way and '*clearly assumes a deliberate act by an individual*'[61] Even if the personal data is in the public domain and it is accessible, it does not always follow that it qualifies for this ground. Controllers will therefore need to consider:

- Whether the data subject actively chose to make the special category data public.

- Whether it has been made public by someone else and if the data subject is aware of the publication.

[59] See: https://ico.org.uk/for-organisations/guide-to-data-protection/guide-to-the-general-data-protection-regulation-gdpr/lawful-basis-for-processing/special-category-data/

[60] See: (https://ico.org.uk/for-organisations/guide-to-data-protection/guide-to-the-general-data-protection-regulation-gdpr/lawful-basis-for-processing/special-category-data/).

[61] See ICO guidance here: https://ico.org.uk/for-organisations/guide-to-data-protection/guide-to-the-general-data-protection-regulation-gdpr/special-category-data/what-are-the-conditions-for-processing/

- Whether the personal data has been put in the public domain in a limited way.

- Whether the personal data has been put in the public domain by default, either due to device or platform settings, or some other process.

The ICO cautions against the use of special category data taken from social media, given the potential difficulty in evaluating the intentions of the data subject. The information may have been put on social media against the wishes of the data subject, or without the knowledge of the data subject. Even if the information was posted by the data subject, the controller cannot know whether default settings made the post more publicly available than intended. According to the ICO, a controller must also consider not whether the personal data is '*theoretically*' in the public domain, but whether it is '*actually publicly available in practice*'. This approach suggests that biometric data, such as a person's image, could qualify as 'manifestly made public' when a person goes about their everyday life and whose image (or other biometric data) is captured through various technological devices.

Substantial Public Interest: UK GDPR Article 9(2)(g)

According to UK GDPR Article 9(2)(g), special category may be processed if it is '*necessary for reasons of substantial public interest, on the basis of domestic law which shall be proportionate to the aim pursued, respect the essence of the right to data protection and provide for suitable and specific measures to safeguard the fundamental rights and the interests of the data subject*'.

Section 10(3) of the DPA 2018 requires processing under this ground to also satisfy one of the 23 specific conditions in paragraphs 6 to 28 of Part 2 of Schedule 1. For most of these conditions it will be necessary to have an 'appropriate policy document' in place.[62] For some of the conditions the controller must also demonstrate that the processing is necessary for reasons of substantial public interest, whereas for others it is 'built' into

[62] Paragraph 5, Part 2, Schedule 1.

the condition, such as the condition of statutory and parliamentary purposes.

The term 'substantial public interest' is not defined in the GDPR, UK GDPR or DPA 2018. The public interest is a concept that appears throughout the law and yet it has no absolute definition. In general, it is approached as a concept that exists to ensure that society's objectives and values are considered, and includes issues such as democracy, the rule of law, public health, the administration of justice, public order, and the effective and transparent working of government. It will also include fundamental rights such as equality and freedom of expression.

The ICO states that organisations relying on this ground must demonstrate its application and cannot include a '*vague or generic public interest argument*'. While there may be a private interest in the processing, the overall purpose of the processing must be of substantial public interest.

Automated Decision Making and Profiling

Automated Decision Making ('ADM') and profiling will become increasingly relevant in the context of biometric data in the future. Big data, machine learning and artificial intelligence are explored further in Chapter IX. As these technological practices develop, it is likely that they will apply ADM and profiling in their processes to some degree.

ADM and profiling are types of data processing that can overlap. ADM which does not have any human involvement in the making of the final decision has particular rules in data protection; it is referred to as 'solely' automated decision making. Whether solely or partly automated, ADM may or may not involve the use of profiles. ADM can involve personal data collected directly from the data subject, observations made about the data subject and derived or inferred data about the data subject.

According to Article 22(1):

> '*The data subject shall have the right not to be subject to a decision based solely on automated processing, including*

> *profiling, which produces legal effects concerning him or her or similarly significantly affects him or her*'.

Whether a decision has a legal effect on an individual is generally straightforward. It is a decision that affects a person's legal status, legal right, or a benefit that is conferred by law. The analysis of whether the processing 'significantly affects' a person, and what the threshold is to come within this description, may be less clear. The European Data Protection Board ('EDPB') suggests that to qualify, the processing must have the potential to:[63]

- Significantly affect the circumstances, behaviour or choices of the individual;
- Have a prolonged or permanent impact on the individual; or
- Exclude or cause the individual to be subject to discrimination.

The ICO suggests that organisations should also consider the extent to which the decision might affect the person's financial circumstances, health, reputation, employment opportunities, behaviour or choices.[64] Typical scenarios where it will be likely to meet the threshold is in the field of employment, health, financial services and education where profiling or ADM may be used to make various decisions or approvals.

If the processing does significantly affect the data subject(s) then it is only permitted where:

---

[63] See the Article 29 Working Party's 'Guidelines on Automated individual decision-making and Profiling for the purposes of Regulation 2016/679', which were revised an adopted by the EDPB on 6 February 2018.

[64] See ICO guidance on ADM and profiling here: https://ico.org.uk/media/for-organisations/guide-to-data-protection/guide-to-the-general-data-protection-regulation-gdpr/automated-decision-making-and-profiling-1-1.pdf

(a) it is necessary to give performance to a contract between the data subject and controller;[65]

(b) It is permitted by law and there are suitable safeguards in place;[66] or

(c) Where the data subject has given explicit consent.[67]

Where (a) and/or (c) apply, the controller must implement suitable safeguards and permit '*at least the right to obtain human intervention on the part of the controller, to express his or her point of view and to contest the decision*'.[68]

Section 14 of the DPA 2018 makes provisions for the safeguards required where ADM is being used under (b) where it results in a 'significant decision'. This is defined in section 14(2) as a decision that 'produces legal effects concerning the data subject' or 'similarly significantly affects the data subject'. A decision is a 'qualifying decision' for this section where it is a significant decision, it is required or authorised by law, and it falls only within Article 22(2)(b) (i.e. not scenarios (a) and (c) above).[69]

If a controller is taking a qualifying decision in relation to the data subject that is solely based on ADM then it must notify the data subject as soon as reasonably practicable.[70] The data subject has one month from receipt of the notification to request the controller to reconsider the decision, or take a new decision that is not based solely on automated processing (that is, involves human input).[71] If the controller receives such a request, it

65 UK GDPR Article 22(2)(a).

66 UK GDPR Article 22(2)(b).

67 UK GDPR Article 22(2)(c).

68 UK GDPR Article 22(3).

69 Section 14(3) DPA 2018.

70 Section 14(4)(a) DPA 2018.

71 Section 14(4)(b) DPA 2018.

has one month to respond; this can be extended to three months if the response is suitably complex. [72]

The controller is obliged to comply with the request and inform the data subject in writing of the steps taken to comply, and the outcome.[73] The EDPB warns that the necessity of human involvement at this stage is involvement by a person that is able to influence the final decision such that the oversight is 'meaningful, rather than just a token gesture'.[74]

Whether the processing for the decision making is solely ADM, or partly ADM (i.e. there is some human involvement in the decision), controllers should provide meaningful information about the logic involved. A complex mathematical breakdown of how the algorithm works is not necessary, but a straightforward explanation should be possible. The EDPB and ICO describe the type of information that would be appropriate as:[75]

- The categories of data that have been, or will be, used in the profiling or decision-making process;
- Why these categories are relevant;
- How any profile is used in the ADM process is created, including any statistics used in the analysis;
- Why the profile is relevant to the ADM process;

---

[72] Section 14(5) DPA 2018 and UK GDPR Article 12(3).

[73] Section 14(5)(b) and (c) DPA 2018.

[74] 'Guidelines on Automated individual decision-making and Profiling for the purposes of Regulation 2016/679', page 21.

[75] Ibid, Appendix 1 and ICO guidance: https://ico.org.uk/media/for-organisations/guide-to-data-protection/guide-to-the-general-data-protection-regulation-gdpr/automated-decision-making-and-profiling-1-1.pdf

- How the profile is used for a decision that concerns the data subject; and

- How it will affect the data subject.

Special Category Data

UK GDPR Article 22(4) prohibits the use of special category data (and therefore biometric data where the individual is to be identified) for solely ADM and profiling unless Article 9(2)(a) or (g) applies and '*suitable measures to safeguard the data subject's rights and freedoms and legitimate interests are in place*'.

Recital 71 GDPR provides further information and context on ADM and describes automatic refusal of an online credit application and e-recruiting as examples where solely ADM produces legal effects. The recital also describes where profiling could do the same, for example where personal data are observed and processed to evaluate personal aspects and to analyse or predict a data subject's '*performance at work, economic situation, health, personal preferences or interests, reliability or behaviour, location or movements*'. In relation to profiling, the recital suggests that the controller should apply appropriate statistical procedures and other measures to ensure that factors which result in inaccuracies are corrected and that the risk of errors is minimised. Controllers should also take steps to prevent any discriminatory effects that could occur as a result of the processing in this context (see '**Best Practice**' below).

Profiling

Article 4(4) of the UK GDPR defines profiling as:

> '*any form of automated processing of personal data consisting of the use of personal data to evaluate certain personal aspects relating to a natural person, in particular to analyse or predict aspects concerning that natural person's performance at work, economic situation, health, personal preferences, interests, reliability, behaviour, location or movements.*'

Profiling involves the collection of information about an individual, or group of individuals, which is then evaluated to categorise individuals. These profiles may then be used to make predictions about a person. A well-known example of this form of processing is in the use of targeted advertising. Data brokers separate consumers into profiles that are relevant to be able to sell to companies. For example, for financial companies, categories such as 'Rural and Barely Making It', 'Ethnic Second-City Strugglers', 'Retiring on Empty: Singles' or scorings based on a person's financial vulnerability are created and sold to them.[76]

Targeted advertising based on profiling may produce significant effects on a data subject, depending on the circumstances and particular characteristics of the data subject. The EDPB states that factors to consider are:[77]

- The intrusiveness of the profiling process (including the extent of tracking across different websites, devices and services);
- The expectations of the data subjects;
- How the advert is delivered; and
- Whether the vulnerabilities of the data subject are targeted (based on data that is directly collected or inferred).

The EDPB cites the example of a high-interest loan being advertised to a person who is known to be in financial difficulties and is therefore more likely to apply for such a loan and incur further debt.[78] Differential pricing based on profiling could also produce significant effects, for

[76] United States Senate Committee on Commerce, Science and Transportation, 'A review of the data broker industry: collection, use and sale of consumer data for marketing purposes, 18 December 2013: http://educationnewyork.com/files/rockefeller_databroker.pdf

[77] Ibid. page 22.

[78] Ibid.

example by offering a prohibitively high price to a person and thereby excluding them from certain goods or services.

A controller must have a lawful basis for processing a data subject's personal data to create a profile on them. The EDPB's view is that it would be difficult for controllers to justify the use of legitimate interests as a basis for profiling for marketing or advertising, where the profiling and tracking is intrusive, or involves tracking across multiple websites, devices, locations, services or data broking.[79] When the controller assesses whether the legal basis of legitimate interests is appropriate, it must also consider the future use or combination of profiles, and the impact that this might have.[80]

The creation of derived, inferred data, or combined data about individuals may create special category data. For example, information about a person's shopping habits, location and age may reveal their state of health. A person's internet browsing habits and places they visit may reveal their political affiliations or beliefs. The Cambridge Analytica scandal illustrates how seemingly innocuous data can be used to identify a person's political persuasion.[81] The conditions under which a controller may process special category data for the purpose of profiling is outlined in the table above in this chapter.

The data protection principle of accuracy is particularly important in the use of personal data in profiling. The EDPB highlights that accuracy is important in all stages of the profiling process: from collection, analysis, creation, to application. Accuracy includes the quality of the personal data being used and ensuring that the dataset is fully representative of the individuals upon which any resulting decision will be based.[82] An incorrect analysis of data could mean that an individual is closed off from

---

[79] Ibid., page 15.

[80] Ibid.

[81] See the House of Commons Digital, Culture, Media and Sport Committee's 'Disinformation and 'fake news': Final Report', 14 February 2019, at: https://publications.parliament.uk/pa/cm201719/cmselect/cmcumeds/1791/1791.pdf

[82] 'Guidelines on Automated individual decision-making and Profiling for the purposes of Regulation 2016/679', page 12.

certain products and services, for example if he or she was placed in the 'Rural and Barely Making It' category, on the basis of an address and/or false inferences.

An organisation must process personal data transparently and is required to provide a data subject with information about how it processes that data (see Chapter III, 'information requirements'). This includes information about profiling.[83] Where the profiling is used for direct marketing purposes, the data subject has an unconditional right to object to profiling.[84]

UK GDPR Article 21(1) gives the data subject the right to object to the processing of their personal data '*on grounds relating to his or her particular situation, at any time to processing of personal data concerning him or her which is based on point (e) or (f) of Article 6(1), including profiling based on those provisions*'. That is, where the processing is relying on the lawful basis of 'public interest' or 'legitimate interests' (see Chapter III). A controller must stop processing the personal data unless it can demonstrate '*compelling legitimate grounds for the processing which override the interests, rights and freedoms of the data subject or for the establishment, exercise or defence of legal claims*'.[85]

There is a difference in the wording of Article 6(1)(f) and Article 21(1) that is relevant where an objection arises. Article 6(1)(f) states as follows: '*processing is necessary for the purposes of the legitimate interests pursued by the controller or by a third party, except where such interests are overridden by the interests or fundamental rights and freedoms of the data subject*'. Whereas the legal basis requires there to be a legitimate interest for which the purpose of the processing is pursued, where an objection arises that legitimate interest must be compelling (my emphasis). This is interpreted

[83] GDPR recital 60.

[84] UK GDPR Article 21(2).

[85] Ibid.

as implying a high threshold to be able to override the data subject's objection.[86]

A controller using a profile on an individual that it has obtained from a data broker should inform the individual about the purposes of the use of the profile and where they obtained the information, and the other information requirements of UK GDPR Article 14 (see Chapter III). Note that if the controller uses the profile as part of a solely ADM process that has legal effects, then it will also be subject to the provisions of UK GDPR Article 22 and section 14 of the DPA 2018 (see above).

A data subject has a right of access to the personal data used to create the profile and may request that any inaccuracies are corrected, or deleted. The view of the EDPB is that a controller should also provide the data subject with information about the profile itself, including the categories or labels attributed to them.[87] This includes the right to rectification and erasure. The data subject may seek to correct or erase both the personal data inputted to create the profile, or the outcome of the use of that personal data, i.e. the profile or scoring itself.[88] A data subject has a right to know the logic involved in any automatic processing of personal data, and when based on profiling, the consequences for him or her.[89]

A controller has the right to protect trade secrets and intellectual property under GDPR recital 63, which states that right of access '*should not adversely affect the rights or freedoms of others, including trade secrets, or intellectual property and in particular the copyright protecting the software*'. However, the recital also states that '*the result of those considerations should not be a refusal to provide all information to the data subject*'.

[86] Guidelines on Automated individual decision-making and Profiling for the purposes of Regulation 2016/679', page 19.

[87] Guidelines on Automated individual decision-making and Profiling for the purposes of Regulation 2016/679, page 26.

[88] Ibid., page 18.

[89] GDPR recital 63.

Best Practice

Appendix 1 of the EDPB 'Guidelines on Automated individual decision-making and Profiling for the purposes of Regulation 2016/679' provides a helpful list of suggestions for controllers to consider when using ADM and profiling. The list is reproduced here:

(1) Regular quality assurance checks of their systems to make sure that individuals are being treated fairly and not discriminated against, whether on the basis of special categories of personal data or otherwise;

(2) Algorithmic auditing – testing the algorithms used and developed by machine learning systems to prove that they are actually performing as intended, and not producing discriminatory, erroneous or unjustified results;

(3) For independent 'third party' auditing (where decision-making based on profiling has a high impact on individuals), provide the auditor with all necessary information about how the algorithm or machine learning system works;

(4) Obtaining contractual assurances for third party algorithms that auditing and testing has been carried out and the algorithm is compliant with agreed standards;

(5) Specific measures for data minimisation to incorporate clear retention periods for profiles and for any personal data used when creating or applying the profiles;

(6) Using anonymisation or pseudonymisation techniques in the context of profiling;

(7) Ways to allow the data subject to express his or her point of view and contest the decision; and,

(8) Mechanism for human intervention in defined cases, for example providing a link to an appeals process at the point the automated

decision is delivered to the data subject, with agreed timescales for the review and a named contact point for any queries.

The EDPB also suggests in Appendix 1 that controllers explore certification mechanisms, codes of conduct for auditing processes and ethical review boards.

Data Protection Impact Assessment

A Data Protection Impact Assessment ('DPIA') is a further safeguard and is necessary '*where a type of processing in particular using new technologies, and taking into account the nature, scope, context and purposes of the processing, is likely to result in a high risk to the rights and freedoms of natural persons*' (UK GDPR Article 35(1)). In particular, where the processing involves:

- A systematic and extensive evaluation of personal aspects relating to natural persons, which is based on automated processing and on which decisions produce legal effects, or significantly affect, the natural person (UK GDPR Article 35(3)(a)).

- Processing on a large scale of special categories of data, or personal data relating to convictions or offences (UK GDPR Article 35(3)(b)).

- A systematic monitoring of a publicly accessible area on a large scale (UK GDPR Article 35(3)(c)).

The EDPB interprets Article 35(3)(a) to include decisions and profiling that do not exclusively use automated processing and it will therefore apply to decision making that may be partly automated.[90]

Article 35(7) sets out the minimum requirements of a DPIA:

[90] 'Guidelines on Automated individual decision-making and Profiling for the purposes of Regulation 2016/679', page 29.

(a) A systematic description of the envisaged processing operations and the purposes of the processing, including, where applicable, legitimate interest pursued by the controller;

(b) an assessment of the necessity and proportionality of the processing operations in relation to the purposes;

(c) an assessment of the risks to the rights and freedoms of data subjects; and

(d) the measures envisaged to address the risks, including safeguards, security measures and mechanisms to ensure the protection of personal data and to demonstrate compliance with the data protection rules.

The DPIA should clearly set out the rights and legitimate interests of data subjects and other persons, and how these have been taken into account by the controller and mitigated against. Where appropriate, and if possible to do without prejudicing commercial or public interests, the controller should seek the views of data subjects.[91] If the processing involves ADM, then the DPIA should identify and record the timing and degree of human involvement in the process.[92]

The ICO states that a DPIA will be required where a controller plans to process special category data to '*determine access to a product, service, opportunity or benefit*' or '*which includes genetic or biometric data (if in combination with any other criteria in European DPIA guidelines)*'.[93] Processing of personal data in innovative technologies or processing which uses biometric data to uniquely identify an individual, or processing that tracks an individual's physical movement or online behaviours will require a DPIA.

---

91 UK GDPR Article 35(9).

92 Ibid., page 21.

93 See ICO guidance on DPIAs: https://ico.org.uk/for-organisations/guide-to-data-protection/guide-to-the-general-data-protection-regulation-gdpr/data-protection-impact-assessments-dpias/when-do-we-need-to-do-a-dpia/?q=genetif#when4.

Where the controller is processing special category data and relying on a condition in Schedule 1 of the DPA, Parts 1 to 3, then it will also be required to have 'an appropriate policy document' in place. For law enforcement, the requirements of the policy document can be found in section 42 DPA 2018. For other controllers where it is necessary, the requirements can be found in Schedule 1, Part 4, paragraphs 39 and 40.

CHAPTER FIVE

CCTV

CCTV in the UK has most commonly been used by law enforcement and in public buildings, businesses, or shops to protect the public and deter crime. However, increasingly CCTV is being used in private homes as surveillance devices are developed and offered to the public with sophisticated capabilities and at relatively low cost. There is no exact figure of how many CCTV cameras are operated in the UK as its use does not have to be registered, but it is estimated by the British Security Industry Association that there up to 5.9 million cameras in the UK. The sophistication of these devices and the ease of use has led to increasing privacy and data protection concerns.

Data Protection

The case of *Ryneš v Úřad pro ochranu osobních údajů C-212/13* decided whether or not CCTV used to protect personal property came within data protection law. In *Ryneš*, the CJEU considered whether the use of CCTV to protect a private home breached data protection law under the Data Protection Directive. For several years, Mr Ryneš and his family and property had been subjected to attacks by unknown persons. He positioned a camera outside his home so that it captured images of his front door, the public footpath and the entrance to the house opposite. In October 2007, his property was targeted again, and using the footage from the camera it was possible to identify two suspects. One of the suspects complained to the data protection authority and Mr Ryneš was found to be in breach of data protection law for not informing persons that they were being filmed by CCTV. Mr Ryneš challenged this decision, and a preliminary ruling was requested of the CJEU on the following:

> *'Can the operation of a camera system installed on a family home for the purposes of the protection of the property, health and life of the owners of the home be classified as the processing of personal data "by a natural person in the course of a purely personal or household activity" for the purposes of Article 3(2) of Directive 95/46 ..., even though such a system also monitors a public space?'*

The Court cited its decisions *Google Spain and Google C-131/12* and *Digital Rights Ireland and Others C-293/12 and C-594/12* emphasizing that the Data Protection Directive is designed to ensure a high level of protection of the fundamental rights in the Charter, in particular the right to privacy with respect to the processing of personal data.[94] Accordingly, derogations and limitations in relation to the protection of personal data must be strictly necessary and therefore the household exemption must be narrowly construed.[95] Given that the CCTV in question recorded a public space, the court concluded it could not be regarded as a 'purely personal or household' activity.[96]

There is no law on image in the UK and as such a private individual has no automatic right to their image to prevent the filming or photographing of them in public by other persons. Challenges to the use or publication of photographs or footage usually falls within privacy law, Article 8 of the Convention and/or breach of confidence. As explained in Chapter IV, under the GDPR images themselves do not fall under the remit of data protection law unless they are being processed for the purpose of identification of an individual. For an image to come within data protection law, it is necessary to consider the context in which it is being processed to determine whether the person in the image is identifiable and that it relates to that person.

Clearly the purpose of CCTV is to identify individuals and so its use is governed by the UK GDPR and DPA 2018 if it does not fall within the household exemption. A private individual, even if using CCTV to

---

[94] The judgment in *Ryneš*, paragraphs 27 and 28.

[95] Ibid., paragraphs 28 and 29.

[96] Ibid., paragraphs 33 and 34.

protect their home, will be considered a controller of personal data if they capture images that go beyond the boundary of their property. The ICO has guidance for domestic use of CCTV on its website, in which it sets out a list of questions to consider in relation to the responsible use of CCTV on private property and whether or not to install it.[97]

Whether using CCTV as a business, or a private individual, the data protection principles must be adhered to (see Chapter III). Most relevant will be to have a legitimate purpose for the use of CCTV (the protection of persons and property would be a relevant and legitimate purpose) and to be transparent. Transparency would be satisfied by having visible signs that notify people that a recording is taking place. However, these two factors alone will not justify the use of CCTV in every scenario. The reach of the CCTV recording and whether or not it is a justified intrusion on the privacy of other people will need to be considered. If there is a less-intrusive method that meets the same objective, then it would be difficult to justify the use of CCTV if it is objected to.

It is also necessary to ensure that the footage is kept securely, deleted at intervals and cannot be accessed or shared by third parties unless permitted by law. Data subjects will also be able to exercise their data rights. Therefore, they can request a copy of CCTV footage of themselves, request footage is deleted and object to the use of CCTV that records them.

Best Practice

The Information Commissioner's CCTV Code of Practice applies to organisations that are deploying a CCTV system and sets out what is considered to be good practice.[98] The Code is still relevant, even though it was published before the GDPR came into effect. It also recommends that the guiding principles in the Surveillance Camera Code ('SCC') are

---

97 ICO guidance available here: https://ico.org.uk/your-data-matters/domestic-cctv-systems-guidance-for-people-using-cctv/.

98 ICO Code of Practice available here: https://ico.org.uk/media/for-organisations/documents/1542/cctv-code-of-practice.pdf

followed and to consider the Protection of Freedoms Act 2012 ('PoFA 2012'), which describes various operational requirements and technical standards.

Organisations are required to follow the CCTV Code to meet their data protection obligations as it sets out recommendations as to how organisations can meet the legal requirements required to do so. The SCC has recently been updated to take into account the Court of Appeal's ruling in the case of *R (Bridges) v The Chief Constable of South Wales Police [2020] EWCA Civ 1058* (discussed in Chapter VII) and is due to come into effect in January 2022.[99] The SCC is relevant to public authorities listed in section 33 of PoFA 2012 in relation to the operation of public surveillance camera systems. While there are no penalties for failing to follow the SCC, a court may take such a failure into account in legal proceedings.[100] Covert surveillance by public authorities is governed by the Regulation of Investigatory Powers Act 2000.

The ICO highlights that '*the fact that it is possible, affordable or has public support should not be the justification for processing personal data. You should also take into account the nature of the problem you are seeking to address; whether a surveillance system would be a justified and an effective solution, whether better solutions exist, what effect its use may have on individuals, and whether in the light of this, its use is a proportionate response to the problem*'.[101]

There may also be situations where the intrusion on the private lives of individuals is such that additional measures to protect their privacy should be applied. For example, if the CCTV covers the entrance to a drug rehabilitation centre, then organisations should consider including

[99] According to the Home Office press release: https://assets.publishing.service.gov.uk/government/uploads/system/uploads/attachment_data/file/1035067/Surveillance_Camera_CoP_Accessible_PDF.pdf

[100] Section 33(4) PoFA 2012.

[101] CCTV Code, page 9.

measures that obscures the image of the faces of those visiting the centre.[102]

The ICO also recommends that a privacy impact assessment is undertaken. For public authorities, depending on the type of processing that is taking place, this may be obligatory, including the requirement for there to be an 'appropriate policy document' in place (see Chapter IV).

The EDPB's guidelines on video surveillance is useful, even if it is no longer binding in the UK.[103] The EDPB highlights how the performance of surveillance systems has changed through the use of intelligent video analysis, which can be more intrusive because of its use of 'complex biometric technologies'. As a consequence, it is becoming increasingly difficult to preserve privacy in public spaces. The EDPB suggests that the legal analysis will differ when using these newer capabilities in surveillance compared with less sophisticated techniques.[104] It also warns that unnecessary surveillance may change cultural norms, leading to the acceptance of a lack of privacy in everyday life.[105]

Data Protection Impact Assessment ('DPIA')

According to Article 35(1) of the UK GDPR a DPIA is necessary where the processing of personal data is '*likely to result in a high risk to the rights and freedoms of natural persons*' and in particular where the type of processing uses new technologies. Where there is '*a systematic monitoring of a publicly accessible area on a large scale*', a DPIA will be necessary.[106] More detail on DPIAs can be found in Chapter IV. The EDPB's view is that CCTV surveillance, in most circumstances, will require a DPIA given that the typical purposes of video surveillance is to protect people, property and to detect, prevent and control the commission of offences

---

102 This is an example given by the ICO on page 16 of the CCTV Code.

103 EDPB 'Guidelines 3/2019 on processing of personal data through video devices – version adopted after public consultation.'

104 Ibid., paragraph 3, page 5.

105 Ibid., paragraph 5, page 6.

106 UK GDPR Article 35(3)(c).

(the latter of which involves the collection of evidence and the use of biometric identification).[107]

Disclosure

One issue that may arise is the question of disclosure of footage from CCTV surveillance. Data sharing is a form of processing and so the requirements of the UK GDPR and the DPA 2018 will need to be met. Namely, a lawful basis for sharing the data in UK GDPR Article 6 and compliance with the data protection principles. Where the transfer of the footage to third parties has the same purpose as obtaining the footage then the same legal basis can apply, although the third party will also have to comply with data protection legislation in its processing of the footage.

The ICO states in the CCTV Code, that where a member of the public has requested footage that may not contain images of the requestor but of other members of the public, then the particular circumstances will need to be considered carefully. The ICO gives the example of a person's car being damaged in a car park and the person requesting footage of the car park in order to provide it to their insurer, or to take legal action. According to the ICO, in such a scenario, '*you should consider whether their request is genuine and whether there is any risk to the safety of the other people involved*'.[108]

Where the request comes from the police, or other regulatory bodies making such a request in order to prevent or detect crime, then disclosure is permitted under UK GDPR Article 6(1)(c). This will also be the case where there is a court order for disclosure of footage.

Where a subject access request is made for footage containing the requestor, which also contains footage of other persons, then unless an exemption to disclosure applies under Schedule 2 of the DPA 2018, the controller will need to comply with the request. Footage of other persons should be obscured so that they are not identifiable. If, however, it is the

[107] EDPB 'Guidelines 3/2019 on processing of personal data through video devices – version adopted after public consultation', paragraph 137, page 33.

[108] CCTV Code, page 15.

identity of other persons that the requestor is seeking, this will need to be considered carefully. The case of *DB v General Medical Council [2018] EWCA Civ 1497* in the Court of Appeal sets out the factors that are relevant when considering whether or not to disclose personal data in 'mixed data' scenarios.

Special Category Data

CCTV may also reveal special category data, which is of a particularly sensitive nature. For example, depending on its location, or observation of a person's habits or journeys, it could reveal information about their health, political opinions or sexual orientation, among others. Whether or not the conditions in UK GDPR Article 9 will apply, depends on whether the data collected from the surveillance system is being used to deduce the special categories and whether the person can be identified.

According to the EDPB, the exemptions in Article 9 are unlikely to apply to justify the use of video surveillance to deduce and collect special category data. Specifically, Article 9(2)(e) – where the exemption applies because the personal data are manifestly made public by the data subject – cannot be used, because the fact that a person is observed by a camera does not imply an intention to make special category data about themselves public.[109] The use of video surveillance which also monitors biometric indicators is covered in the chapters on facial recognition technology and emotion recognition.

Remedies

As explained in Chapter III, to obtain solutions to data protection issues individuals may complain to the ICO and/or start civil proceedings. The ICO website has a form for CCTV-specific complaints at: https://ico.org.uk/your-data-matters/domestic-cctv-systems-guidance-for-people-being-filmed/i-m-unhappy-about-the-use-of-a-home-cctv-system-what-can-i-do/y/Unable/No/Yes. However, the ICO states that '*in most CCTV-related disputes between neighbours, the ICO will not consider it appropriate or proportionate to take enforcement action against*

[109] EDPB 'Guidelines 3/2019 on processing of personal data through video devices – version adopted after public consultation,' paragraph 70, page 17.

the CCTV user'. Therefore, for most disputes between neighbours, unless matters can be resolved between the parties, or the police are involved (in serious disputes), then civil proceedings will be the likely course of action to come to some sort of resolution.

Case Law

Data Protection

Fairhurst v Woodward Case No. G00MK161, County Court Oxford, 12 October 2021

This was a recent case that was much publicised in the UK press and was a neighbour dispute involving the use of CCTV. The claimant, Dr Mary Fairhurst, and the defendant, Mr Jon Woodward, were neighbours in a row of terraced houses. Their cars were parked in spaces that were behind their gardens. The defendant had installed multiple devices to protect his property. These included:

- A floodlight and sensor on his garden shed at the back of his garden, which overlooked the parking spaces ('the Floodlight').

- A video and audio surveillance camera with an integrated motion sensitive spotlight (Amazon's 'ring' spotlight camera system) located on the shed pointing at the parking spaces ('the Shed Camera').

- A combined video and audio surveillance system on his front door (Amazon's 'Ring' video doorbell) ('the Ring Doorbell').

- On another neighbour's back garden wall facing the car park a Ring spotlight camera ('the Driveway Camera').

- A 'Nest' camera inside his front windowsill pointing out towards the front of the property ('the Windowsill Camera').

The timings of the installations and whether the defendant had informed the claimant were contested, but the judge concluded that the Shed Camera and Ring Doorbell had been installed in 2018. Further, it was found that the defendant had told the claimant that these devices were not capable of capturing images or data of the claimant. On 25 April 2019, a group of three men attempted to steal the defendant's car. The Shed Camera captured the incident, which the Judge was able to view at trial. The men were dressed in black and wearing hats. The defendant called 999 and the police attended his property. After the incident he installed the Driveway Camera in addition to the Shed Camera.

On 28 April 2019 the claimant noticed the additional camera. She spoke with a neighbour who told her she had seen footage from the Driveway Camera as the defendant had shown it to her. From the angle of the Driveway Camera, the claimant's garden wall and gate and foliage in her garden could be seen. The claimant contacted the defendant to object to the cameras on the basis that it was an intrusion of her privacy and those of her visitors. A number of events took place after the initial objection which formed the basis of the claimant's harassment claim against the defendant. At trial the judge found the following acts by the defendant to have constituted harassing behaviour:[110]

(i) He falsely told the claimant that he had sent footage of her to the police, when he saw a 'suspicious' person near his car but had not recognised her, in an attempt to intimidate her.

(ii) Statements made in phone calls on 29 April 2019 where he deliberately tried to scare the claimant. For example, saying that through the cameras "*he had everything covered now*" and that there was "*nothing you can do*".

(iii) Threatening in a text message to report the claimant's friend to the police when her friend had been inspecting the cameras.

(iv) A threat to install more cameras, including concealed cameras (which ultimately resulted in the claimant leaving her home).

(v) A conversation with the claimant's friend on 8 May 2019 in which the defendant made various further threats, such as

[110] Paragraph 126, page 41 of the judgment.

installing more surveillance, and told him that he was an expert in such equipment and could "*hack things*".

(vi) The lies told to the claimant, including that the cameras were non-operational 'dummy' cameras.

In relation to the data protection claim, the judge reviewed the technical capabilities of the various devices. The Shed Camera and Driveway Camera were manufactured by Ring. According to the manufacturer's specifications, they were '*battery-powered high definition motion-activated video security cameras with a wide-angle lens, built-in motion-activated spotlight, infrared night vision, built-in microphone and speakers, two-way audio facility and a 110-decibel alarm*'.[111] The device sends motion-activated alerts to a mobile phone, tablet, computer or smart watch in the form of a 30-second video clip and can also provide live video and audio feeds through an app.[112]

The CCTV warning sign that the defendant placed at the front and back of the property simply stated: "*WARNING Concealed CCTV cameras operate on these premises*". The judge accepted the claimant's evidence that the wording and presence of the sign felt intimidating to her, given the threats that had been made.[113] The field of view was140 degrees horizontal.[114] The Ring Doorbell had similar capabilities, but with a wider field of view of 155 degrees horizontal.[115]

The manufacturer of these devices has since changed their capabilities, but at the time the defendant had been using them it was not possible to operate the video without using the audio function as well. The Ring Doorbell could capture audio at a distance of about 68 feet (21 metres) and was activated at about 17 feet (5 metres) from the door. The Shed

---

[111] Ibid., paragraph 89, page 29.

[112] Ibid.

[113] Ibid., para 87, page 28

[114] Ibid., para 91, page 30

[115] Ibid.

Camera could record audio at a range of a maximum of about 53 feet (16 metres).

The judge concluded from the maps and diagrams provided in evidence that the specifications meant that the defendant's Ring doorbell would be activated by anyone walking along the pavement in front. The judge found that it was probably also activated by passing cars on the road. Once activated, it would be able to record audio at the claimant's front door, in the pavement in front of her house and on part of her driveway.

The Driveway Camera viewed the claimant's garden wall, part of her garden, her gate, and part of the car park that she or her guests would enter and leave. It did not include any area that formed the defendant's property and would be activated by any car or person entering or leaving the car park, any person leaving a car parked in the claimant's parking space and by the use of the claimant's gate. All of these areas were covered by the camera's audio function.

The Shed Camera captured a large area of the car park and was not focussed only on the defendant's car. It included the top of the driveway and the claimant's car parking spaces. It would be activated by any car leaving the car park and by pedestrians in the car park. The audio function would cover a large area such that conversations in the car park, the top of the driveway and the claimant's car parking spaces could be heard.

There was less evidence on the Windowsill Camera, and the judge concluded that it did not capture any images of the claimant (unless she approached the defendant's front door), or her property, and was not considered further.

The defendant was found to be in breach of the first data protection principle, in failing to be fair and transparent, as he had actively misled the claimant about the capabilities of the cameras. He was also found to be in breach of the second data protection principle because he '*has not collected the data for a specified or explicit purpose but rather sought to mislead the claimant*'.[116]

The defendant relied on the basis of legitimate interest for processing the personal data and submitted that the surveillance was '*necessary for the purposes of crime prevention at his property and in the car park*'.[117] The Judge found that the use of the Driveway Camera was not necessary for this legitimate aim as it only collected data that was outside his property and his car parking spaces were not within its field of vision. The Shed Camera too captured video and audio that were beyond the boundaries of his property. Further, it was found that his cars could be protected in a less intrusive way, for example by using a camera that only had his cars in view.[118]

In relation to all the devices, the judge found the audio capabilities to be particularly problematic and more detrimental to a person captured in the footage than the video data.[119] In particular it was noted that '*the extent of the range means that personal data may be captured from people who are not even aware that the device is there, that it records and processes audio personal data, or that it can do so from such a distance away*'.[120] She concluded that the collection of audio data failed the data minimisation principle and in addition '*cannot be said to be reasonable for the purpose for which the devices are used by the defendant, since the legitimate aim…namely crime prevention, could surely be achieved by something less*'[121]. The defendant was concluded to be in breach of the UK GDPR and DPA 2018 in his use of home surveillance.

---

[116] Ibid., paragraph 133, pages 45 to 46.

[117] Ibid., paragraph 134.

[118] Ibid., paragraph 135.

[119] Ibid.

[120] Ibid., paragraph 137.

[121] Ibid.

Anthony and Deborah Woolley v Nahid Akbar [2017] Scot SC 7

This was another neighbour dispute involving CCTV. The 'pursuers' ('claimants') lived in their family home in Edinburgh in the top flat of a semi-detached house. The 'defender' ('defendant') owned the flat below theirs and ran it as a guest house, which was managed by her husband Mr Akram. At the front of the house there was a car parking area. To the rear there was a garden which was divided in half by a fence. The claimants' access to their garden was via a pathway to the side of the house. The defendant's portion of the garden was accessed through a basement door at the rear of the house. Neither party had access to the other's garden area.

In 2013 the relationship between the parties deteriorated. Both parties installed CCTV systems. The claimants attached cameras to the outer wall of their property which records images of their external property: part of the car parking area, the pathway and stone access staircase to their external door, and their garden area. The defendant attached a surveillance system to the external wall of her property which records both video and audio data and operated 24 hours each day. After five days, new data recorded over the past recordings. The data could be remotely accessed.

The claimants argued that from October 2013, the defendant's CCTV was deliberately arranged to cover their private property and that Mr Akram knew this but did not take any measures to ensure this was minimised or avoided. In effect, the claimants and every person approaching the claimants' home would be recorded. This included their private garden area.

The evidence submitted showed that the defendant's audio surveillance installed (four audio boxes) could pick up private conversations in the claimants' garden. One was also installed immediately below the claimants' front bedroom windows and from which they feared they could be heard within their home. On one occasion Mr Akram '*taunted the pursuers about his ability to listen to them as the pursuers conversed in their garden*'.[122]

The court found that the defendant had failed to give notice, consult them or provide any information when the surveillance was installed. Visitors to the property were also not informed of the surveillance or the fact that it recorded both video and audio. The defendant had failed to respond to requests from the claimants for information, or copies of the coverage of the surveillance. The claimants complained to the ICO, but the defendant told the ICO that the premises were her own private residence.

It was concluded that '*the data processing by the defender's system is intrusive, excessive and unjustified. It is unnecessary in relation to any legitimate purpose*'.[123] The methods deployed were described as '*oppressive*' and the lack of information and response was unfair; the defendant was found to be in breach of the first, third and fifth principles of data protection.[124]

The judge noted the '*considerable distress*' the claimants had experienced as a result of the surveillance that had prevented them using their garden and '*severely restricted ... the use and enjoyment of their own home*'.[125] The surveillance had caused them to voluntarily restrict their external movements and conversations and they had to warn their visitors about the surveillance. The claimants sought £10 per day for the intrusion of the surveillance and were awarded, on this basis, a total of £8,634 with interest.

ICO Investigations

The most recent and high-profile investigation into CCTV by the ICO was announced in July 2021 after 'The Sun' newspaper published footage of politician Matt Hancock having an affair. The footage came from

---

[122] Paragraph 7 of the judgment.

[123] Ibid., paragraph 10.

[124] Ibid.

[125] Ibid., paragraph 13.

CCTV in Mr Hancock's office. The ICO is investigating the alleged personal data breach, which involved the Department of Health and Social Care ('DHSC') CCTV footage and EMCOR Group (UK) plc. EMCOR provides the facilities management and CCTV services for DHSC and it is alleged that the footage was taken from the CCTV system without the consent of either EMCOR or DHSC.

There is currently an ongoing criminal investigation into whether there was a breach of section 170 of the DPA 2018, which criminalises '*knowingly or recklessly obtaining, disclosing or procuring personal data without the consent of the controller, or selling or offering for sale that personal data*'.[126]

Privacy and Human Rights

Privacy law may also be relevant if images or videos of a person, or their home or family are published or used without their consent and where there is a reasonable expectation of privacy. A person's image has been found to engage Article 8 of the Convention. It was noted by the ECtHR in the case of *Reklos and Davourlis v Greece Application No 1234/05, 15 January 2009* that:

> '*a person's image constitutes one of the chief attributes of his or her personality, as it reveals the person's unique characteristics and distinguishes the person from his or her peers. The right to the protection of one's image is thus one of the essential components of personal development and presupposes the right to control the use of that image*'.[127]

It is possible therefore, that where CCTV footage is being used in such a way that it amounts to a misuse, a claim in misuse of private information may be brought. Against a public body, it may be possible to bring a human rights claim under the Human Rights Act 1998 ('HRA 1998')

---

[126] ICO statement at: https://ico.org.uk/about-the-ico/news-and-events/news-and-blogs/2021/07/statement-on-ico-investigation-into-department-of-health-and-social-care-cctv-footage/

[127] At paragraph 40 of the ruling.

for breaches of the Convention, either of Article 8 of the Convention and/or for breaches of other Convention rights. Principle 2 of the SCC states that '*the user of a surveillance camera system must take into account its effect on individuals and their privacy, with regular reviews to ensure its use remains justified*'. The principle acknowledges the potential effects on Article 8, the freedom of thought, conscience and religion (Article 9 of the Convention), freedom of expression (Article 10 of the Convention), freedom of assembly and association (Article 11 of the Convention) and protection from discrimination (Article 14 of the Convention). Following the decision in *R (Bridges)* the updated SCC includes reference to the need to take particular account of the Public Sector Equality Duty and the necessity of a DPIA (see Chapter VII).

Cases

The majority of privacy claims to date have been in relation to photographs, but by extension, the same principles would apply to video footage. The following cases involved CCTV.

In the matter of an application by JR38 for judicial review (Northern Ireland) [2015] UKSC 42

The appellant was 18 years old at the time of the judgment of the Supreme Court. It was before Lord Kerr, Lord Clarke, Lord Wilson, Lord Toulson and Lord Hodge.

On 23 and 26 July 2010, two newspapers in Ireland published an image of the appellant at the request of the police when he was 14 years old. A photograph of him was published, alongside images of others, who had been involved in public disorder in Londonderry. The police were operating a Campaign known as 'Operation Exposure' to counteract sectarian rioting in boundary parts of Derry. Images of rioters were taken from CCTV that had been taken at the time of the riots.

The appellant had been interviewed by police on 1 July 2010 about his involvement in the rioting on 24 May 2010 and 8 June 2010 and was shown CCTV footage of both incidents. He claimed to be able to identify himself from the footage, but it was disputed whether he identified himself in the image that was later published. The respondent asserted that at that stage the appellant had not been identified.

The Supreme Court noted that the appellant had been involved in offences other than the rioting in question. He had been arrested for riotous behaviour in August 2009, charged with two separate offences of rioting in 2010, and charged with possession of an offensive weapon. The police gave evidence about the increasing tensions in areas of Derry and that community representatives had informed the police that they had lost control over the youths, who were becoming increasingly violent.[128]

At public meetings in June and July 2010 between the police, local councillors and community representatives the issue was discussed, and it was agreed that the violence had to be stopped. The chief inspector informed the attendees that it was necessary to identify the youths involved in the rioting and presented photographs of the rioters. None was identified and a period of two weeks was set to allow identification in private meetings before it would be published in the newspapers.

Operation Exposure involved various stages of inquiry; the publishing of CCTV images was not automatic. It began with the investigating officer reviewing the individual offences and then pursing conventional lines of enquiry, such as recording statements from complainants, witnesses and suspected offenders. Before making public use of CCTV footage or photographs, the officer was required to take reasonable steps to identify a suspect by less intrusive means, such as door-to-door inquiries, circulation among other police officers and other forensic examination. There was also an authorisation procedure before release could take place. This was set out in a guidance document and included the consideration of human rights issues. Where children were concerned, there were additional considerations, including whether there is a risk to the young person from the community and where their best interests lie.

The appellant argued that the publication of his image violated his Article 8 Convention right. The Divisional Court in Northern Ireland dismissed his application for judicial review and he appealed to the Supreme Court.

[128] Paragraph 11 of the judgment.

The question for the Supreme Court was whether the publication of the photographs of the appellant constituted a breach of his Article 8 Convention right.

The Supreme Court unanimously agreed that the appeal should be dismissed and that the second part of the two-stage test when considering an Article 8 claim had been met. That is, that the interference with private life was justified in the circumstances. The following points were concluded in relation to necessity and proportionality:

- The objective of Operation Exposure was to detect and prevent crime, bring to justice those who were guilty of committing criminal offences, prevent sectarian violence and divert young people from crime, all of which are necessary in a democratic society;[129]

- Physically pursuing youths at the time of riots was not feasible as the youths could outrun the police who were in heavy riot protection equipment;[130]

- The police had a 'painstaking approach' to identifying the offenders before relying on making CCTV stills public, which was 'truly a measure of last resort';[131]

- The sectarian violence put many vulnerable people at risk, including the young persons involved in the violence themselves;[132]

- There is a need to protect children from the risk of both criminalisation and stigmatisation;[133]

---

[129] Ibid., paragraphs 71 and 73.

[130] Ibid., paragraph 74.

[131] Ibid., paragraphs 76 and 77.

[132] Ibid., paragraph 77.

[133] Ibid., paragraph 78.

- It is in the interests of the claimant that he is diverted from criminal activity and become a law-abiding citizen in his community;[134] and

- The operation was successful in reducing the number of interface confrontations and overall violence.[135]

Their Lordships disagreed on the question of whether the first part of the Article 8 test was met. The differing judgments on this point are worth reading to see the approaches to the question of whether or not Article 8 is engaged when the applicant is engaged in a criminal offence. In particular, their Lordships differed in their view on how 'reasonable expectation' should be approached, what importance should be placed on it to determine whether Article 8 is engaged, and how the fact that a child is involved alters the analysis.

In relation to the data protection element of the claim, their Lordships concluded that there had not been a breach of the DPA 1998. The photograph was 'sensitive personal data' under section 2(g) DPA 1998. As a data controller, the police were required to comply with the data protection principles but under section 29 DPA 1998 were exempt from the first data protection principle if processing personal data for:

(a) the prevention or detection of crime,

(b) the apprehension or prosecution of offenders...

Insofar as it requires compliance with Schedules 2 and/or 3, which related to the processing of sensitive personal data. As the police were processing the personal data for the administration of justice, the conditions in the schedules were met. Therefore, no breach was found to have taken place and the publication was in accordance with data protection law. Note that this exemption is mirrored in the DPA 2018 at Schedule 1, Part 2, paragraph 10.

---

134 Ibid., paragraph 79.

135 Ibid., paragraph 80.

Peck v United Kingdom (44647/98) 28 January 2003

This case involved the publication of images from CCTV footage by the media of a man attempting to commit suicide. In 1994, Brentwood Borough Council ('the Council') installed a CCTV surveillance system in Brentwood. In 1995, Mr Geoffrey Peck was suffering from depression and one evening walked out into the streets of Brentwood carrying a kitchen knife in his hand, and cut his wrists. He stopped at a junction and was recorded by a CCTV camera mounted on a traffic island. The police were notified by the operator of the CCTV, who arrived on the scene, took the knife from him and took him to be treated by a doctor. The police released Mr Peck without charge.

The next month, the Council authorised the release of the footage as part of a press feature about CCTV use by them. The press feature showed two photographs taken from the footage, with the title "Defused – The partnership between CCTV and the police prevents a potentially dangerous situation". Mr Peck's face was not obscured. After the press release, a number of local newspapers published articles using the photographs. Later, Anglia Television was given the footage by the Council and included it in a local news broadcast, although Mr Peck's face was obscured at the Council's request.

However, the masking was inadequate, and Mr Peck could be recognised by those who knew him. Shortly after the broadcast his neighbour told him that he had featured in a television broadcast. At around the same time, the Council released the footage to the BBC to be used on the programme 'Crime Beat', which attracted a viewership of some 9 million people. Although the Council imposed conditions, including masking, again, the technique applied was insufficient and he was identifiable.

Mr Peck applied for judicial review of the Council's decision to disclose the CCTV material arguing that it was unlawful. This was rejected on the basis that disclosure was permitted under section 111 of the Local Government Act 1972 and section 163 of the Criminal Justice and Public Order Act 1994 to promote the prevention of crime. His appeals were dismissed and he applied to the ECtHR, arguing that the disclosure constituted a disproportionate interference with his Article 8 Convention right.

The ECtHR highlighted that the Council had failed to use other options that were available to achieve the same objectives.[136] For example, it could have identified the applicant through enquiries with the police and obtained consent for the disclosure. Alternatively, the Council could have sufficiently masked the image of the applicant in the footage before disclosing it to the media. The court also pointed out the failure of the Council to obtain written obligations from the media to sufficiently protect the identity of the applicant.[137] It was noted that Mr Peck had not committed a crime and had not been charged with any crime.

A violation of Article 8 of the Convention was found. The ECtHR concluded that there were insufficient reasons to justify the direct disclosure of Mr Peck's image to the media and that there had been insufficient safeguards put in place to guarantee his right to respect for private life.

---

[136] Paragraphs 80 to 81 of the judgment.

[137] Ibid., paragraph 83.

CHAPTER SIX

DRONES

Drones are unmanned flying aircraft that range from small lightweight models, more akin to toys, to heavier aircraft with sophisticated abilities. Drones are currently used in many different industries, such as in emergency search and rescue operations, medicine delivery and to inspect infrastructure and construction.[138] There are many potential applications of drones, such as precision farming, the monitoring of environmental changes, fire detection, communications, and weather monitoring. Companies such as Amazon.com Inc. and Alphabet Inc. (Google's parent company) are already developing drone delivery services.

In the UK, a government consultation on drones was conducted in 2018. The purpose was to evaluate the current legislation governing drones to address misuse, but also to examine how the commercial drone sector is likely to develop and to obtain views on drone detection technology.[139] The Department for Transport, the Department for Business, Energy and Industrial Strategy, and the Home Office are together considering product standards for drones. A large proportion of commercial drones include geo-fencing capabilities to prevent them flying in certain areas and the Government is engaging with manufacturers to improve these safeguards.[140] The European Aviation Safety Agency is currently drafting new drone product standards, which includes geo-fencing.

In December 2018, Gatwick airport in the UK was closed three times in three days, leaving 110,000 passengers stranded because of alleged drones within the air space of the runways.[141] The increasing private use of

---

138 See 'Taking Flight: The Future of Drones in the UK', Secretary of State for Transport, January 2019.

139 Ibid., pages 25 and 26.

140 Ibid, paragraphs 1.27 and 22.

141 BBC News, 'Gatwick Airport: Drones ground flights', 20 December 2018 at https://www.bbc.co.uk/news/uk-england-sussex-46623754).

drones, and the incident at Gatwick airport, led the Government to pass legislation to address their use. In 2019, a number of regulations were introduced to restrict the use of drones in populated areas.[142]

The technology is fast developing, and it is already possible for drones to apply facial recognition technology to identify an individual from above. 'Smart' drones have been available since 2015.[143] Drones that are fitted with cameras or sensors that collect personal data will have implications for data protection and privacy, depending on how and where they are used. This book examines data protection and privacy considerations in the use of new technologies and an analysis of the rules that govern the operation of drones goes beyond its scope.

However, the relevant legislation to examine would be:

- The Air Traffic Management and Unmanned Aircraft Act 2021, which received royal assent in April 2021 and provides police with the authority to address the misuse of drones.
- The Air Navigation Order 2016 (SI 2016/765).
- Commission Implementing Regulation (EU) 2019/947.
- Commission Delegated Regulation (EU) 2019/945.[144]

And further regulatory guidance can be found on the Civil Aviation Authority website, specifically:

- CAP722, Unmanned Aircraft System Operations in UK Airspace.

---

[142] For example, the Air Navigation (Restriction of Flying)(The Oval, London) Regulations 2019/608

[143] The US company 3D Robotics created 'Solo', the world's first 'smart' drone. See: https://3drobotics.com/company/about-3dr/

[144] The two EU regulations have been retained in UK law after Brexit through the Unmanned Aircraft (Amendment)(EU Exit) Regulations 2020 (SI 2020/1593).

- Drone and Model Aircraft Code.

Data Protection and Privacy

There are no specific rules that govern drones in the GDPR, UK GDPR and DPA 2018. Drone users have to register with the Civil Aviation Authority and obtain training, unless the drones being used are classified as toys and do not have a camera. Those persons operating small toy drones as a hobby, without capturing images, will be exempt from the obligations of data protection law. However, individuals operating drones that are able to capture photographs or video are unlikely to be able to rely on the 'household exemption' for the reasons given in the *Ryneš* judgment (see Chapter V). Therefore, the use of drones will have the same considerations as the use of CCTV, in particular where they are used for surveillance purposes.

There are few cases involving drones, and as yet no cases relating to data protection and privacy. However, two cases that could be relevant in the future are *Bernstein of Leigh v Skyviews & General Ltd [1978] 1 QB 479* and *Fearn and others v The Board of Trustees of the Tate Gallery [2019] EWHC 246 (Ch).*

In *Bernstein Leigh*, the claimant brought a claim in trespass and invasion of the right to privacy against an aerial photography company that had flown over his home to take photographs, which it later tried to sell to him. The law did not permit the pursuit of 'invasion of privacy' (the tort of misuse of private information had not yet been developed) and only trespass was considered. Mr Justice Griffiths found for the defendant on the basis that the airspace above Lord Bernstein's home, at the height the plane had been flown, did not interfere with the ordinary use and enjoyment of his land and could not constitute a trespass. The defendant had only taken a single photo, but Griffiths J commented that hypothetically, had the claimant suffered from constant surveillance from the air, '*such a monstrous invasion of his privacy*' could be actionable in nuisance.

In *Fearn and others v The Board of Trustees of the Tate Gallery*, Mr Justice Mann suggested at first instance, that the tort of nuisance was capable of protecting privacy rights. The case involves the residents of a block of flats in London, who live in a new development called 'Neo Bankside', which is adjacent to the Tate Modern museum. Their living areas are mostly glass and look directly onto a new extension on the museum called 'the Blavatnik', which includes a viewing gallery on the top level. The viewing gallery wraps around the Blavatnik, permitting a 360 degree viewing capability. From the viewing gallery it is possible to see directly into the claimants' flats. The claimants brought a claim against the Tate Modern in privacy under the HRA 1998 and Article 8 of the Convention, and nuisance.

The case failed on the HRA 1998 claim because the judge concluded that the Tate Modern was not considered a public authority for the purposes of the Act. However, Mann J found that '*privacy is an aspect of the amenity of land*' and that the Courts are obliged to develop the law to give effect to Article 8 of the Convention pursuant to the HRA 1998.[145] Mann J highlighted the extension of the cause of action of breach of confidence to accommodate Article 8 of the Convention in *Campbell* and concluded that the law of nuisance ought to be capable of protecting privacy rights from being overlooked in appropriate cases.[146]

On the facts, the claimants did not succeed in their claim for nuisance. To succeed they had to prove that the amenity, or utility, of their property had been interfered with to the detriment of the property itself, such that they should not have to put up with it, even on the 'give and take' basis that is expected in neighbourly relations.[147] It was found that the design of their properties was such that they would expect a degree of exposure and that they could take steps to improve their privacy.

The Court of Appeal affirmed the decision of Mann J, but for different reasons.[148] On the question of whether the cause of action for private

---

145 Paragraph 128 of the judgment.

146 Ibid., paragraphs 174 and 175.

147 The principle of 'the reasonable user' as described by Lord Goff in Cambridge Water Co. v Eastern Counties Leather plc [1994] 2 AC 264, and Lord Millett in Southwark London Borough Council v Tanner [2001] 1 AC 1.

148 *[2020] EWCA Civ 104.*

nuisance could be extended to incorporate a breach of Article 8 of the Convention, the Court of Appeal disagreed because:

(1) An objective test in nuisance for determining whether there has been a material interference with the amenity value of the land from 'overlooking' would be difficult to achieve;[149]

(2) The tort of nuisance protects damage to interests in property and there are other laws available to protect privacy, namely misuse of private information, confidentiality, data protection, harassment and stalking;[150]

(3) Any extension of the law in this area is better suited to intervention by the legislature;[151]

(4) The fusion of the tort of private nuisance with Article 8 would '*significantly distort the tort in some important respects*' given that the tort is a property tort and does not give licensees cause of action;[152]

(5) Factors that are relevant to assessing a reasonable expectation of privacy are irrelevant to the cause of action of nuisance, such as the particular sensitivity of the claimant;[153] and

(6) The assessment of justification under Article 8(2) is also difficult and at odds with the tort of private nuisance.[154]

The claimants appealed to the Supreme Court; the appeal was heard in December 2021 and as yet judgment has not been delivered. The two issues considered were:

---

149 Ibid., paragraph 81.

150 Ibid., paragraph 84.

151 Ibid., paragraph 84.

152 Ibid., paragraph 91.

153 Ibid., paragraph 92.

154 Ibid., paragraph 93.

(1) Whether the Court of Appeal erred in failing to hold that private nuisance, understood in light of the requirements of section 6(1) of the HRA 1998, is capable of providing a remedy against 'viewing' from neighbouring land.

(2) Whether public viewing from the viewing gallery into the flats infringes their rights under Article 8(1) of the Convention.

The outcome of this case could be relevant for the use of drones in the future. The Court of Appeal approached the claimant's objections as one of 'overlooking', however the issues they described was that they felt constantly watched, that the interior of their homes could be observed and that photographs had been posted on social media that commented on this fact. Should the Supreme Court conclude that privacy can be incorporated into the tort of private nuisance, individuals objecting to drone use could have a further cause of action upon which to rely.

Best Practice

The Civil Aviation Authority's guidance outlined above should be referred to when operating, designing and/or manufacturing drones. In relation to data protection, the Article 29 Working Party's 'Opinion 1/2015 on Privacy and Data Protection Issues relating to the Utilisation of Drones' sets out a number of practical recommendations. There are particular issues that drones pose to privacy. For example, the unique vantage point of drones, the effectiveness of any on-board sensors and reduced transparency due to the difficulty a data subject will have in observing them.[155]

The processing of images of individuals, property, vehicles, geolocation data, and electromagnetic signals that relate to an individual by equipment on a drone will fall within data protection legislation.[156] It is likely that the fact that this sort of personal data is being collected by a drone will not be known to data subjects, or even if the drone is obvious,

[155] Article 29 Working Party's 'Opinion 1/2015 on Privacy and Data Protection Issues relating to the Utilisation of Drones', 16 June 2015, page 5.

[156] Ibid., page 7.

they will not know why their personal data is being collected, and by whom. This could create *'an increased feeling of being under surveillance'* with a consequential chilling effect on the exercise of civil liberties.[157] For this reason it is essential that drone operators ensure that they implement 'data protection by design and default', which is a requirement under UK GDPR Article 25.[158]

In its Opinion, the Article 29 Working Party identifies 'steps to be taken before operating a drone' and makes recommendations to manufacturers and/or operators, which are reproduced in the tables below.

Steps to be taken before operating a drone
1. Check if the national law allows operating drones and verify the need for a specific authorization from the civil aviation authorities; 2. Clarify the roles of possible different actors: as far as the processing is not carried out directly by the controller, ensure that the processing is governed by a contract or legal act binding the processor to the controller and that the processor acts only on instructions from the controller; 3. Evaluate the data protection impact taking into account the purpose of the operations and the type of drones (dimension, visibility, etc.) and the specific combinations of sensing technology on-board it; identify the most suitable legal basis (consent of the data subjects, performance of a contract, legal obligation, legitimate interest, etc.) and the possible need to

[157] Ibid.

[158] For more about this concept, see my blog article 'The GDPR's 'Data Protection by Design and Default', 28 January 2020 at: https://privacylawbarrister.com/2020/01/28/the-gdpr-data-protection-by-design-and-default/

notify/consult the competent data protection authorities according to national data protection law;

4. Choose the most proportionate technology on-board and adopt all suitable measures of privacy by default: set services and products in such a way as to avoid the collection and/or the further processing of unnecessary personal data;

5. Find the most appropriate way to give advance notice to those who can be impacted by the data processing: inform through signposts or information sheets in case of visual operation in a specified area; in case of an event, inform public by means of social media, newspapers, leaflets or posters; give clear information always on the relevant website: the information notice should contain a clear indication of the controller and the purposes of the processing and should give data subjects clear and specific indications for exercising the right to access visual and non-visual records concerning them;

6. Take all the appropriate technical and organisational measures to ensure a level of security appropriate to the risks represented by the processing and the nature of the data to be protected, in particular, to prevent any unauthorised processing also during the "transmission" phase;

7. Delete or anonymise any unnecessary personal data soon after the collection or as soon as possible.

Recommendations to manufacturers and/or operators

1. Embed privacy friendly design choices and privacy friendly defaults as part of a privacy by design approach;

2. Involve a Data Protection Officer (where available) in the design and implementation of policies related to the use of drones;

3. Promote and adopt Codes of conduct that can help the industry and different categories of operators prevent infringements and enhance the social acceptability of drones; such Codes should contain sanctions in case the signatories do not comply with the code;

4. Make the drone as far as possible visible and identifiable (using emitted wireless signal, flashing lights or buzzers, bright colours);

5. When in line of sight, make the operator clearly visible and identifiable with signage as the individual responsible for the drone;

6. When planning and operating a flight, even where allowed to operate the drone over populated areas, avoid as far as possible to fly over or near private areas and buildings.

CHAPTER SEVEN

FACIAL RECOGNITION

The development of facial recognition and detection technology began in the 1960s. The technology has rapidly advanced in the past few decades due to the massive leap in computing power and the near inexhaustible supply of digitized imagery on the Internet. This has enabled facial recognition technology to develop at a rapid pace, particularly in the private sector.[159]

There are distinctions to be understood in the terminology. Facial detection is where technology is used to determine whether an image contains a face. Facial analysis is when the technology is used to identify attributes such as gender, age, ethnicity, or emotion. Facial recognition compares a person's facial features to available images on a database to identify a person. Live facial recognition is where the technology is deployed in a public space in 'real time'. For the purposes of this chapter, I shall refer to facial detection and recognition collectively as 'FRT'.

There is no specific law in the UK that governs the use of FRT. For the development of FRT by commercial organisations, the relevant legal considerations will generally be intellectual property, data protection and potentially, privacy law. If FRT is applied in advertising, compliance with the Directive on Privacy and Electronic Communications 2002/58/EC and the Privacy and Electronic Communications Regulations 2003 will also be necessary.

---

[159] For example, Apple Inc.'s iphone uses a face detection system to unlock and car manufacturers such as Subaru and Jaguar Landrover are developing facial analysis systems to detect fatigue or the driver's 'mood'. See https://www.subaru.com.au/driver-monitoring-system and https://media.jaguarlandrover.com/news/2019/07/car-responds-your-mood-new-jaguar-land-rover-tech-helps-reduce-stress. It has also, controversially, been developed for use in schools to allow cash-less payments for lunch, see: https://www.crbcunninghams.co.uk/news/crb-cunninghams-launch-facial-recognition-to-uk-schools

In the public sector, the same considerations apply, except where FRT is also being used to make decisions, then public law actions could be relevant. For the public sector it is also necessary to comply with the public sector equality duty to promote equality and, as a public body, they need to act in a manner compatible with the Convention rights. The focus of this book is on data protection and privacy, which has so far been the main approach to challenging the use of FRT.

Data Protection

As outlined in chapter IV, where a person's image is being used to identify a person, it will fall within the definition of biometric data for the purposes of UK GDPR Article 9(1). FRT will usually come within this definition and the additional conditions and safeguards for processing will therefore apply. There may be circumstances where facial detection technology is being applied without the element of identification. For example, it may be deployed to detect a face and analyse the age of a person, but not their identity. In some industries, the technology is also being developed to analyse emotions, this is sometimes referred to as 'empathic' or 'empathetic' technology and is discussed in Chapter VIII.

The approach in the UK to FRT differs from Europe, where there is a reticence to adopt the technology in law enforcement as quickly as it has been considererd in the UK. The European Parliament voted on 6 October 2021 to ban the use of FRT in public spaces by law enforcement, until there are technical standards in place to ensure it does not compromise fundamental rights. The rapporteur emphasized the need for further societal debate and the implementation of several core principles in the development of AI (see Chapter IX on AI).[160]

The most significant case in the UK and one of few globally that has addressed the question of live automated FRT is *R (Bridges) v The Chief Constable of South Wales Police [2020] EWCA Civ 1058*. The decision was unanimous and agreed with the applicants that the use of the

---

160 European Parliament, 'Report on artificial intelligence in criminal law and its use by the police and judicial authorities in criminal matters 2020/2016 (INI)', 13 July 2021.

technology by the police was in breach of Article 8 of the Convention. However, the court did not find that the use of live automated FRT was in itself the problem. In principle, it did not contravene data protection rules, but the way it had been applied had left too much discretion to the police, had failed to apply clear criteria, and had not considered the potential bias in the software. This case is reviewed more fully below as it is an important judgment for this technology.

R (Bridges) v The Chief Constable of South Wales Police [2020] EWCA Civ 1058

The Appellant was Edward Bridges, a civil liberties campaigner. The Respondent was the Chief Constable of the South Wales Police ('South Wales Police'). South Wales Police had been given funding by the Government to develop automated FRT in policing. It had a licence to use proprietary software called 'NeoFace Watch', which was developed by North Gate Public Services (UK) Ltd.

The software worked in stages. Using a database of existing facial images, a 'watchlist' was created. These were the faces that the system operator wanted to find in a crowd. The images were processed so that particular features were extracted and assigned numerical values to create a unique biometric template. Next, a CCTV camera would take digital pictures of facial images in real time. The software detected human faces from the live feed and isolated individual faces. It then automatically extracted unique facial features from those images and created a unique biometric template for each face. The software compared the 'new' templates made from those created from the live feed, against the existing templates in the watchlist. During the comparison, the software generated a 'similarity score', which is a numerical value indicating the likelihood that the faces match. A threshold value was fixed to determine when a match had occurred.

The South Wales Police used the software around 50 times between May 2017 and April 2019, mostly at large public events. It referred to this use as 'AFR Locate'. CCTV cameras were mounted on police vehicles, poles or posts. To inform the public about the use of AFR Locate, the South Wales Police put messages on Facebook and Twitter, displayed large notices on the police vehicles, handed out postcard notices to members of the public and put information on its website.

The watchlists were created from images held on the South Wales Police database, mostly custody photographs. The purpose of the watchlists was to find persons wanted on warrants, those who had escaped from custody, criminal suspects, missing persons or people in need of protection, persons of interest for intelligence purposes and individuals whose presence at a particular event might cause concern. If during the deployment of AFR Locate, the software identified a possible match, the two images were then reviewed by a police officer, and action taken if necessary. The system could scan 50 faces per second and the total number it could scan was unlimited.

If no match was made when comparing two images, the live scanned image and its associated biometric template were immediately and automatically deleted. The CCTV feed was deleted after 31 days. If a possible match was alerted, the image was deleted either immediately or within 24 hours and the match report was deleted after 31 days. Newly created watchlist images and the associated biometric templates were deleted either immediately, or within 24 hours of deployment.

Mr Bridges was contesting two occasions when AFR Locate was used when he was present: on 21 December 2017 on a busy shopping street in Cardiff, and on 27 March 2018 at a Defence Exhibition. At the first occasion, AFR Locate had used three watchlists, in all comprising some 900 persons. There were 10 possible matches, two of which were assessed not to be true matches. Two arrests were made.

At the second occasion, three watchlists were used to seek out suspects and persons wanted on warrants. One of the watchlists comprised a list of persons who had been arrested at the same event the previous year, including one who had made a false report of a suspected bomb. That person was identified by AFR Locate but no action was taken. No arrests were made.

Even though both these events occurred whilst the DPA 1998 was in effect, the parties requested that the court should consider them under the DPA 2018.

The Grounds of Appeal

There were five grounds of appeal. The appellant argued that the Divisional Court had erred in making the following conclusions:

(1) That the use of automated FRT was in accordance with the law for the purposes of Article 8(2) of the Convention;

(2) That the use of automated FRT was a proportionate interference with Article 8 of the Convention, in particular in failing to consider the cumulative interference with the Article 8 Convention rights of all the people whose facial biometrics were captured during the deployments;

(3) That the DPIA for the use of automated FRT complied with section 64 DPA 2018. The appellant argued that the DPIA failed to take into account Article 8 of the Convention, and the processing of biometric data of those persons not on the police watchlists;

(4) That it declined to conclude whether the South Wales Police force has in place an 'appropriate policy document' within the meaning of section 42 DPA 2018, taken with section 35(5) DPA 2018; and

(5) That it held that the respondent had complied with the Public Sector Equality Duty ('PSED') in section 149 of the Equality Act 2010 in circumstances in which the respondent's 'Equality Impact Assessment' was obviously inadequate because it failed to recognise the risk of indirect discrimination.

The Judgment

(1) Ground 1: 'In accordance with the law' for Article 8 of the Convention

The underlying question under this ground was whether there was a sufficient legal frame framework for the use of AFR locate. The general principles to evaluate the 'in accordance with the law' standard are well established (Lord Sumption in *R(Catt) v Association of Chief Police Officers [2015] UKSC 9* and in *Re Gallagher [2019] 2 WLR 509*) and are summarised as follows:

- The measure in question must have some basis in domestic law and must be compatible with the rule of law, which means it should comply with the requirements of 'accessibility' and 'foreseeability'.[161]

- To be accessible, the legal basis must be published and comprehensible, and it must be possible to find out what the provisions are.[162]

- To be foreseeable it must be possible for a person to foresee its consequences. It should not confer a discretion so broad that in practice, its scope depends on the will of those that apply it, rather than the law itself.[163]

- The law must clarify the scope of the discretion, and the manner of its exercise by competent authorities to guard against arbitrariness.[164]

- Where the measure is a discretionary power, it need not be over-rigid in its application, but there must be safeguards to guard against 'overbroad discretion resulting in arbitrary, and thus disproportionate, interference with Convention rights'.[165]

- The rules governing the scope and application of the measure need not be statutory, provided that they operate within a framework of law with an effective means of enforcing them.[166]

---

[161] *Sunday Times v United Kingdom (1979) 2 EHRR 245; Silver v United Kingdom (1983) 5 EHRR 347; Malone v United Kingdom (1984) 7 EHRR 14.*

[162] Lord Sumption, *Re Gallagher [2019] 2 WLR 509* at [17].

[163] Ibid.

[164] *S v United Kingdom, ibid,* at [95] and [99].

[165] Lord Hughes in *Beghal v Director of Public Prosecutions [2016] AC 88'* at [31] and [32].

[166] Lord Sumption in *R(Catt) v Association of Chief Police Officers [2015] UKSC 9* at [11].

The Divisional Court found that there was a clear and sufficient legal framework governing AFR Locate found in the provisions of the DPA 1998 and 2018, the Surveillance Camera Code, and the South Wales Police force's own policy documents. Those policies, according to the Divisional Court, could be 'altered and improved' over the course of the trial of AFR Locate, and this did not indicate that the policy documents were deficient. The Court of Appeal disagreed: *'We find the references by the Court to the possibility of future reconsideration of this issue a little curious. This is because either an interference is in accordance with the law or it is not... The fact that this case involved the trial of a new technology does not alter the need for any interference with Article 8 rights to be in accordance with the law'.*[167]

The Court of Appeal highlighted the significance of the fact that automated FRT is a novel technology and that it involves the collection of 'sensitive' personal data within the meaning of the DPA 2018; it goes beyond the taking of a photograph or the use of CCTV. Whilst stating that a 'large part' of the Divisional Court's analysis was correct, the judgment pointed to some 'fundamental deficiencies' described as the '*who question*' and the *'where question'*.[168] The Court of Appeal was of the view that there was too much discretion left to police officers to determine who was placed on the watchlist, and that there were no clear criteria on where AFR Locate could be deployed.

The DPA 2018 was concluded to provide an '*important part of the framework in determining whether the interference with the Appellant's Article 8 rights was in accordance with the law*', but is not by itself sufficient.[169] The Information Commissioner was of the view that the processing was not based on law within the meaning of section 35(2) DPA 2018, interpreted in accordance with the EU Law Enforcement Directive and the Convention, because there was no legal basis for its application that was clear, precise and foreseeable. However, as this

---

[167] Paragraph 58 of the judgment.

[168] Ibid., paragraphs 85 to 91.

[169] Ibid., paragraph 104.

particular point was not raised by the Appellant, the Court of Appeal did not make any conclusions on this issue.

The Court of Appeal noted the inclusion of facial recognition within parts of the Surveillance Camera Code of Practice that was issued by the Secretary of State for the Home Department in June 2013. It was of the view that the problematic 'who' and 'where' questions could in principle be dealt with in a revised Code.[170]

On the matter of the South Wales Police force's local policies, the Court of Appeal evaluated the 'privacy impact assessment' under the DPA 1998, the DPIA under the DPA 2018 and its 'Standard Operating Procedure'. All were found to be lacking in relation to the questions of who could be placed on a watchlist and where the deployment of AFR Locate could take place. The appeal was therefore allowed on this ground.

(2) Ground 2: Proportionate interference

Whether an interference with Article 8(1) of the Convention is proportionate is determined by the four-part test in *Bank Mellat v Her Majesty's Treasury (No 2) [2014] AC 700*:

(i) Whether the objective of the measure pursued is sufficiently important to justify the limitation of a fundamental right;

(ii) Whether it is rationally connected to the objective;

(iii) Whether a less intrusive measure could have been used without unacceptably compromising the objective; and

(iv) Whether, having regard to these matters and to the severity of the consequences, a fair balance has been struck between the rights of the individual and the interests of the community.

The Appellant argued that the Divisional Court had been wrong in its conclusions on the fourth question on two aspects. First, the 'benefit' part of the proportionality balance must take into account both 'actual'

[170] The SCC has been revised to take into account this judgment, see Chapter V.

results (in this case, the number of arrests) and its 'anticipated' benefits. Second, that the 'cost' part of the proportionality balance does not only take into account the particular appellant, but all the members of the public whose Article 8 Convention rights have been interfered with by deployment of AFR Locate. This argument was rejected by the Court of Appeal on the basis that the interference with another member of the public was analogous to the situation of the Appellant and in any event, there was no such cumulative effect such that the impact on Article 8 becomes 'weightier'.[171]

(3) Ground 3: Compliance with section 64 DPA 2018

Three criticisms were made of the DPIA. First, it contained no recognition that automated FRT entails the processing of the personal data of persons not on the watchlist. Secondly, it did not acknowledge that the Article 8 Convention rights of those persons are engaged. Thirdly, it did not engage with the issue of the risks to other rights that are likely to be affected by the use of automated FRT, such as the right to freedom of assembly under Article 11 of the Convention and to freedom of expression under Article 10 of the Convention.

The Information Commissioner too criticised the DPIA, highlighting that it had failed to acknowledge that it involves the collection of data *'on a blanket and indiscriminate basis'* and had not addressed the potential for gender and racial bias, or considered the effects of a false positive match.[172] The Court of Appeal found that some of these criticisms were unjustified, in that the DPIA had acknowledged that automated FRT '*might be perceived as being privacy intrusive in the use of biometrics and facial recognition and that Article 8 of the Convention was relevant*'.[173] However, it agreed that the DPIA had proceeded on the basis that Article 8 of the Convention was not infringed, and given the Court's conclusions on whether its use was 'in accordance with the law' to satisfy the

---

[171] Ibid., paragraph 143.

[172] Ibid., paragraphs 148 and 149.

[173] Ibid., paragraph 151.

requirements of Article 8(2) of the Convention, the DPIA did not comply with Article 64 DPA 2018.

The Court of Appeal concluded: *'notwithstanding the attempt of the DPIA to grapple with the Article 8 issues, the DPIA failed to properly assess the risks to the rights and freedoms of data subjects and failed to address the measures envisaged to address the risks arising from the deficiencies we have found, as required by section 64(3)(b) and (c) of the DPIA 2018'*.[174]

(4) Ground 4: Compliance with section 42 DPA 2018

Section 42 DPA 2018 sets out what 'an appropriate policy document' should contain for the purposes of processing sensitive data for law enforcement purposes under section 35(5) DPA 2018. The Divisional Court had left open to question whether the South Wales Police 'November 2018 Policy Document' fully met the standard required on the basis that the Information Commissioner had provided further guidance. The Court of Appeal rejected this ground on the basis that the two events under consideration (in December 2017 and March 2018) took place when the DPA 1998 applied, not the DPA 2018.

(5) Ground 5: The Public Sector Equality Duty 'PSED'

The terms of the PSED are found in section 149(1) of the Equality Act 2010. In this case, the relevant protected characteristics are race and sex. The Appellant criticised the failure of the South Wales Police to consider the scientific evidence that bias can be found in facial recognition software such that there is a greater risk of false identifications for people from Black, Asian and other Minority Ethnic backgrounds, and for women. Further, it was argued that the PSED is an ongoing obligation, and that the Respondent was in continuing breach of it.

The Court of Appeal concluded that this point is *'a serious issue of public concern, which ought to be considered properly by [the Respondent]'*.[175] It noted the relevant legal principles in relation to the PSED were set out

---

[174] Ibid., paragraph 153.

[175] Ibid., paragraph 172.

by McCombe LJ in *R (Bracking) v Secretary of State for Work and Pensions [2013] EWCA Civ 1345*:[176]

(1) The PSED must be fulfilled before and at the time when a particular policy is being considered;

(2) The duty must be exercised in substance, with rigour, and with an open mind. It is not a question of ticking boxes;

(3) The duty is non-delegable;

(4) The duty is a continuing one;

(5) If the relevant material is not available, there will be a duty to acquire it and this will frequently mean that some further consultation with appropriate groups is required; and

(6) Provided the court is satisfied that there has been a rigorous consideration of the duty, so that there is a proper appreciation of the potential impact of the decision on equality objectives and the desirability of promoting them, then it is for the decision maker to decide how much weight should be given to the various factors informing the decision.

The Court of Appeal agreed that the PSED is a *'duty of process and not outcome'* and *'helps to reassure members of the public, whatever their race or sex, that their interests have been properly taken into account before policies are formulated or brought into effect'*.[177] A public authority is required to proactively consider whether to alter its practices and structures in order to meet its statutory duty to promote equality and eliminate discrimination.[178] This positive duty requires a public authority not to inadvertently overlook information that it should take into account. The Court was critical of the failure of the South Wales Police to independently verify that the NeoFace Watch software algorithm was not

[176] At paragraph 60 of the judgment in *R(Bracking)*.

[177] Ibid., paragraph 178.

[178] Ibid., paragraphs 177 to 178.

biased towards a particular group and said that the fact that AFR Locate was in its trial stage did not change the requirement to discharge its duty.

ICO Investigations

In July 2020, the ICO and the Office of the Australian Information Commissioner ('OAIC') opened a joint investigation into Clearview AI Inc., a company based in the United States ('U.S.'). The company had scraped billions of images of people's faces from the Internet to create a facial recognition search application.[179] The application allowed a person to enter a person's image and it would then be matched, using a 'webcrawler', with associated information about the person on the Internet (such as social media information), so that they could be identified. The company had offered its services only to government and law enforcement, but its international patent application listed private sector applications, such as identifying a person for business or dating, or granting access to venues.[180]

Clearview was found by the regulators to have collected the personal information of millions of people of which '*only a fraction … would ever be connected with law enforcement investigations. The evidence shows that this included the information of vulnerable individuals, including victims of crime and children*'.[181] Clearview allegedly wanted to accumulate 30 billion images of people by 2020.[182] The OAIC concluded that the company had committed serious breaches of data protection laws.

In November 2021, the ICO announced its provisional intent to impose a fine of just over £17 million for the breaches of data protection law

179 OAIC decision 'Clearview AI, Inc. (Privacy) [2021] AICmr 54 (14 October 2021).

180 Ibid., paragraph 7.

181 Ibid., paragraph 178.

182 Ibid., paragraph 61.

found in the joint investigation.[183] The ICO concluded that Clearview had:

- Failed to process personal data fairly and in a way that people would expect;
- Failed to have a process in place to stop personal data being retained indefinitely;
- Failed to have a lawful reason for collecting the information;
- Failed to meet the higher data protection standards required for biometric data;
- Failed to inform people in the UK about how their personal data was being used; and
- Asked for additional personal information, including photos, from individuals who objected to their data being processed, which may have acted as a disincentive to individuals seeking to exert their data protection rights.

The ICO also issued a provisional notice to Clearview to stop any further processing of the personal data of persons in the UK and to delete any such personal data held by the company.[184] Clearview may make further representations in respect of the ICO's conclusion and a final decision is expected in mid-2022.

[183] ICO press release, 29 November 2021, available here: https://ico.org.uk/about-the-ico/news-and-events/news-and-blogs/2021/11/ico-issues-provisional-view-to-fine-clearview-ai-inc-over-17-million/

[184] Ibid.

Best Practice

ICO Opinion 'The use of live facial recognition technology in public places', 18 June 2021

The ICO published an opinion on the use of live facial recognition technology ('LFRT') in public places in June 2021.[185] The opinion highlights common failings of controllers in the development and application of LFRT such as:

(1) Where controllers rely on vendor's LFRT products but do not fully understand how those products work, or fully appreciate their legal obligations.[186]

(2) To clearly identify its justification that the automatic and indiscriminate processing of biometric data is necessary and proportionate.[187]

(3) Failing to adopt a 'data protection by design and default' approach.[188]

(4) Failing to sufficiently consider the effectiveness of LFRT in achieving their objective against the potential impact on data subjects in DPIAs.[189]

(5) Insufficient transparency measures, in particular the display of signage, communications to the public, and the information available in privacy notices.[190]

---

185 Available here: https://ico.org.uk/media/2619985/ico-opinion-the-use-of-lfr-in-public-places-20210618.pdf

186 Page 11 of the ICO's Opinion.

187 Ibid., page 19.

188 Ibid., page 20.

189 Ibid.

190 Ibid.

(6) Not making it clear to data subjects how and why their data is being processed and how they can exercise their rights.[191]

(7) A lack of due diligence in respect of the technology purchased from manufacturers, including a failure to scrutinise the accuracy and '*presenting accuracy rates without clear understanding of their provenance or suitability to the controller's proposed use case*'.[192]

(8) 'Watchlists' being used that do not always comply with data protection law and are not maintained in a lawful, fair and transparent way.[193]

The Opinion outlines the following practices as necessary to be compliant with data protection law:[194]

Necessity and Objectives
Controllers must demonstrate that the processing is necessary and that they have considered and ruled out less intrusive options.[195]
LFRT must not be deployed simply because it is available, improves efficiency, reduces costs or is part of a particular business model.[196]
Controllers must properly consider whether their objective is sufficiently important to justify the processing of biometric data and interfere with an individual's privacy.[197]

[191] Ibid.

[192] Ibid., page 21.

[193] Ibid.

[194] The Opinion provides detailed guidance and should be read in full.

[195] Page 53 of the ICO's Opinion.

[196] Ibid.

[197] Ibid., page 36.

Controllers must properly consider whether a fair balance has been struck between its own interests against the rights of the individual and the community.[198]
Bias and Discrimination
Controllers must balance the risk of bias and discrimination and ensure fair treatment of individuals in both the application of LFRT and in the creation of watchlists.[199]
Controllers must identify and take steps to mitigate against the risk of bias and discrimination.[200]
Controllers must consider the risk of bias, discrimination and unfairness during the design, commission or procurement process of any LFRT system.[201]
Data Protection by Design and Default
Controllers must adopt a data protection by design and default approach.[202]
Controllers must consider the direct or indirect impact on individuals' fundamental rights in a public setting, such as freedom of expression, assembly and association.[203]

198 Ibid.

199 Ibid.

200 Ibid., page 39.

201 Ibid.

202 Ibid., page 46.

203 Ibid., page 44.

Controllers must ensure any products or services purchased from vendors have been designed with data protection and privacy-preserving features built-in as controllers have ultimate responsibility under data protection law.[204]
Diligence
Controllers should ensure that the LFRT system has been subject to robust testing in their decisions and processes.[205]
Controllers should monitor the outcomes of the LFRT system, including for any evidence or bias or discrimination and adapt their approach accordingly.[206]
Watchlists
Controllers must strictly limit the images that are included on the watchlist to those which are necessary and proportionate and must only retain watchlists for as long as is necessary.[207]
Watchlists should only include lawfully acquired images that are accurate and with identifiable provenance; the ICO considers images sourced from social media as being of uncertain provenance.[208]

[204] Ibid., page 46.

[205] Ibid., page 39.

[206] Ibid., page 39.

[207] Ibid., page 47.

[208] Ibid., pages 47 and 48.

Data Subject Rights
Controllers must ensure that any products or services purchased from vendors are capable of giving effect to a data subject access request unless valid exemptions apply.[209]
Data subjects must be able to exercise their data subject rights in relation to watchlists, including their right to be informed, to rectification, to erasure and to object to the processing.[210]
Data subject rights apply to any watchlist data shared with third parties and any other records held by controllers.[211]
Data Sharing
Where collaborating with law enforcement, controllers must ensure that the roles and responsibilities are clear with appropriate governance and accountability measures and that the specific legal requirements of the UK GDPR and DPA 2018 are met.[212]
Any exemptions under the UK GDPR and DPA 2018 relied upon in the sharing of watchlist data must be necessary and proportionate and clearly justified.[213]
DPIA
The ICO sets out what it expects to see in DPIAs for the application of LFRT in public places in the annex to the Opinion.[214]

[209] Ibid., page 46.

[210] Ibid., page 21.

[211] Ibid.

[212] Ibid., page 52.

[213] Ibid., page 21.

[214] Ibid., pages 56 to 67.

Council of Europe 'Guidelines on Facial Recognition', 28 January 2021

In January 2021, The Council of Europe adopted new guidelines on facial recognition that provides recommendations to both the public and private sector.[215] There are three sections in the guidelines:

- Guidelines for legislators and decision makers
- Guidelines for developers, manufacturers and service providers
- Guidelines for entities using facial recognition technologies

While these guidelines have been recently developed, it is important to remember that the regulatory landscape for the use and application of FRT is rapidly changing and any reliance on the guidelines should be adopted within this context. Many data supervisory authorities in EU Member States are proposing bans on the use of FRT in public spaces, in particular for the use of advertising.[216] Globally, there have been a number of legal challenges to the use of FRT, including in Sweden, Belgium and the US.[217]

Future Developments

The UK House of Lords Justice and Home Affairs Committee began an inquiry into new technologies in law enforcement in July 2021. The committee will examine the existing legal framework, the ethical issues that arise in their use and whether advanced algorithms in law

---

[215] The Consultative Committee of the Convention for the protection of individuals with regard to automatic processing of personal data (Convention 108), 'guidelines on facial recognition', June 2021, available here: https://rm.coe.int/guidelines-on-facial-recognition/1680a134f3

[216] For example, the Norwegian Data Protection Commissioner Bjørn Erik Thon has called for a ban on surveillance-based advertising.

[217] I have summarised these legal challenges in a journal article: 'Facial Recognition and Detection Technology: Developments and Challenges', Communications Law Journal (2020) Vol 25, No 3.

enforcement produce reliable and consistent outputs.[218] There is also currently a bill in the House of Lords that proposes to make it a criminal offence to '*operate, commission or install*' equipment that incorporates automated FRT that is capable of analysing the biometric data of individuals in the public.[219]

Further changes will also be on the horizon in Europe. In April 2021, the European Commission proposed a 'Regulation for Artificial Intelligence' (see Chapter IX). The proposed regulation would apply to FRT, categorising different systems by their level of risk, and impose certain requirements depending on that risk.

---

218 House of Lords Justice and Home Affairs Committee, press release dated 22 July 2021, available here: https://committees.parliament.uk/committee/519/justice-and-home-affairs-committee/news/156778/call-for-evidence-launched-on-new-technologies-in-law-enforcement/

219 Automated Facial Recognition Technology (Moratorium and Review) Bill [HL]: https://publications.parliament.uk/pa/bills/lbill/58-01/087/5801087.pdf, currently in its second reading in the House of Lords.

CHAPTER EIGHT

EMOTION RECOGNITION

There are a number of other technologies that are being developed using physiological and behavioural data, which have so far attracted less attention in the courts and from regulators. However, as the use of our biometric data in a variety of applications expands, so too it is likely that the issues that have been identified by the ICO and by the court in *R (Bridges)* will arise. In particular, FRT is being developed further to include an examination of emotion to provide an analysis of 'sentiment'. This is sometimes referred to as 'empathic' or 'empathetic' technology. It may also involve a combination of biometric data and facial analysis to try and measure human emotion.[220] It is anticipated that this type of technology will have future application in the provision of personalised services, advertising, education, medical diagnosis, public safety and crime detection.[221]

This type of technology will also have relevance in the gaming industry and in the 'metaverse'. The metaverse does not have a legal definition but it is a term used to describe the culmination of a number of technologies that create an 'alternative reality' or virtual place where individuals can interact. For example, it includes virtual reality, online games accessed through computers or consoles, and the digital economy, where products and services are bought and sold. It is seen as an additional augmented layer to the real world.

Companies such as Apple Inc., Microsoft Corporation and Meta Platforms Inc. (Facebook's parent company) are all investing in different

---

220 European Parliamentary Research Service, 'Regulating facial recognition in the EU', September 2021, page 4.

221 European Data Protection Supervisor, TechDispatch 'Facial Emotion Recognition', Issue 1 2021: https://edps.europa.eu/system/files/2021-05/21-05-26_techdispatch-facial-emotion-recognition_ref_en.pdf

aspects of the metaverse. Apple has 14,000 augmented reality apps available on its augmented reality development platform.[222] Microsoft is making a number of acquisitions to grow its gaming business portfolio.[223] Meta has filed multiple patents in the U.S. to use biometric data, in particular related to facial expressions, in applications that the company intends will enhance a user's experience in the metaverse.[224]

Legal Challenges and Objections

As yet, there have been few challenges to emotion analysis technology. This is unsurprising given that the technology is at present in its development stage and has not been deployed to any great extent. In the next decade however this is likely to change, given the significant investment that is being made globally in the technology sector and the generational interest and demand for virtual products and services.

Patrick Breyer v European Research Executive Agency, Case T-158/19, 15 December 2021

In Europe, there has been an objection to the exploration by state authorities of emotion technology, without adequate transparency to the public. Patrick Breyer, a Member of the European Parliament and a digital rights activist, has been seeking the disclosure of information from a trial project involving 'deception detection'. In 2016, the EU Horizon Research Programme gave around 4.5 million to the company

---

[222] Apple Inc. January 2002 quarterly earnings call: https://www.apple.com/investor/earnings-call/

[223] See Microsoft's press release, 18 January 2022: https://news.microsoft.com/2022/01/18/microsoft-to-acquire-activision-blizzard-to-bring-the-joy-and-community-of-gaming-to-everyone-across-every-device/

[224] This was first reported by the Financial Times on 19 January 2022 'Facebook patents reveal how it intends to cash in on metaverse'. One example is patent number 10277893, 'characterization of optical distortion in a head mounted display', United States Patent and Trademark Office.

iBorderCTRL for a pilot project using its face-matching and 'automated deception detection' software at airports.[225]

iBorderCTRL has developed technology that it claims can detect when someone is lying from their facial expression.[226] Using the software, travellers would be questioned by border control staff, and those that were flagged by the system would be given more detailed screening. The principal idea was that the system would speed up border crossing and offer more thorough checks.

In 2018, Breyer made a freedom of information request to the European Commission's Research Executive Agency ('REA') for the ethical assessments and trial outcomes of the project.[227] He was concerned about reports that the technology creates a high proportion of false positives.[228] The REA resisted disclosure of all the documents on the basis that it prejudiced the commercial interests of the consortium.[229] Breyer challenged this decision and in November 2019, the CJEU rejected the Commission's request for the case to be dismissed.

In December 2021, the grand chamber of the CJEU considered the request and agreed that there is a public interest in knowing about the future application of surveillance systems and therefore, the results of a pilot test would come within the obligation to disclose such information under freedom of information laws.[230] Further, it was of the view that '*there is an interest of the public in participating in an informed public and democratic discussion on the desirability of control technologies such as those*

225 EU Commission Horizon 2020 Factsheet: https://cordis.europa.eu/project/id/700626

226 According to iBorderCTRL's technical framework, see https://www.iborderctrl.eu/Technical-Framework

227 Patrick Breyer v European Research Executive Agency, Case T-158/19, 15 December 2021, paragraph 4.

228 See Patrick Breyer's website: https://www.patrick-breyer.de/?p=590076&lang=en

229 Paragraphs 5 and 7 of the judgment.

230 Ibid., Paragraph 199.

at issue and whether they should be funded by public money, and that this interest must be duly protected'.[231]

The CJEU did not go so far as to order the disclosure of all the documents requested, on the basis that there was no particular urgency that overrode the legitimate interest in protecting the commercial interests of the consortium in relation to some of the documents.[232] However, it did require REA to disclose the following documents that had previously been refused:[233]

- The Ethics advisor's first report.
- Documents on the ethics of profiling, the risk of stigmatization of individuals and the mitigation plan.
- Information on the ethics advisor.
- The requirement analysis report.
- The reference architecture and components specification.
- The specifications of the data collection devices.
- The dissemination and communication plans.

The documents that the court decided could remain confidential are:

- The quality management plan (containing information on project management, planning of technical means and delivery of results).

[231] Ibid., paragraph 200.

[232] Ibid., paragraph 202.

[233] Ibid., paragraph 204.

- Periodic progress reports (containing descriptions of technological progress on different aspects of the project).

- Annual reports (containing descriptions of technological progress on different aspects of the project).

Best Practice

The ICO has not published any specific guidance on empathic technology, although many of the data protection considerations in its use would mirror those found in *R(Bridges)*, in particular in its application by law enforcement. The ICO's guidance on LFRT will be relevant to organisations who are developing applications using this technology, particularly in a real-time public setting (see Chapter VII). The IEEE, a not-for-profit technology organisation, currently has a working group to develop a global standard for the ethics of empathic technology. The standard will define a model for ethical considerations and practices in the design, creation and use of empathic technology and aims to provide practical guidance to developers to protect users from bias or exploitation.[234]

Organisations should be mindful that the technology has been criticized for the lack of strong scientific evidence to support the proposition that it is possible to determine what people are thinking, feeling, or intending by measuring facial expression.[235] The ICO has highlighted in its LFRT guidance that it expects controllers to demonstrate the accuracy of the technology that is being applied (see Chapter VII). Even if characteristics are being measured and recorded without the intention of identifying a person, the types of information are likely to fall within the broad definition of personal data in data protection law, unless truly anonymised.

---

[234] IEEE P7014 Emulated Empathy in Autonomous and Intelligence Systems Working Group, 'Standard for Ethical considerations in Emulated Empathy in Autonomous and Intelligent Systems'.

[235] See the 'Report of the United Nations High Commissioner for Human Rights A/HRC/48/31', 13 September to 1 October 2021, paragraph 28.

The European Data Protection Supervisor ('EDPS') highlights the problem of achieving data accuracy in the application of empathic technology (referred to by the EDPS as 'facial emotion recognition technology'). Facial expressions vary between individuals and may not reveal any emotional state at all. Factors such as the context and the conditions in which the expression is taking place and variations in socio-cultural expression and mannerisms could lead to further ambiguity.[236] Where the results of empathic technology are used in applications that affect a data subject, if the inputted results cannot be shown to be accurate, the controller will be likely to be in breach of the fourth data protection principle.

The accuracy of the conclusions of the empathic analysis could also have implications for the principle of fairness. An inaccurate or flawed analysis could lead to discrimination against people of a particular race, or societal group. For example, the EDPS notes that in one study, it was shown that some facial emotion recognition algorithms assign more negative emotions to people of colour, than to other faces.[237] Of concern is the possibility that information derived from empathic technology may be shared and used by other entities, such as employers or insurance companies, without the knowledge or consent of the data subject.[238] The use of this type of technology could also lead to individuals adjusting their behaviour over time, once they are aware they are being observed.[239]

There is a difference between recording a person's mannerisms in order to create a realistic avatar of them in the metaverse and using that same data to infer information about them. The EDPS has advised that '*turning human expressions into a data source to infer emotions touches clearly a part of people's most private data*'.[240] Depending on the context

[236] European Data Protection Supervisor, TechDispatch 'Facial Emotion Recognition', Issue 1 2021, page 3.

[237] Ibid., citing: Rhue, Lauren (2018). Racial Influence on Auto- mated Perceptions of Emotions. In: SSRN Electronic Journal. doi: 10.2139/ssrn.3281765.

[238] Ibid., page 4.

[239] The EDPS warns that this could create a feeling of insecurity and would have a chilling effect on society as a whole.

[240] Ibid., page 2.

and circumstances in which this type of data is collected, if it could be classified as a misuse, it could also form the basis of a misuse of private information claim. The collection of information related to a person's emotions without their consent or knowledge, is likely to be information that a person could expect would remain private.

CHAPTER NINE

ARTIFICIAL INTELLIGENCE

Artificial intelligence ('AI') is the ability of computers or machines to perform intelligent tasks such as solving complex problems and making decisions and predictions based on an analysis of data. The term 'AI' is in fact a reference that currently describes the processing of algorithms in machine learning. As yet, 'artificial general intelligence' or 'general purpose AI' – when machines surpass human intelligence – has not been achieved.[241] For the purposes of this chapter, I shall refer to 'AI' to mean the application of algorithms by computers, machines, and devices, although many different definitions of AI exist.

AI has rapidly advanced in recent years, due to the availability of massive amounts of digital information (so-called 'big data') and the increase in computer processing power. It is particularly relevant to new technologies and biometric data. AI is likely to transform societies and economies in the coming decades. Globally, the way in which AI is developed and deployed will have an enormous impact on our lives, both positive, and potentially negative.

---

[241] The achievements of the chess-playing computer Deep Blue and game-playing computer AlphaGo are considered examples of 'Artificial Narrow Intelligence' rather than 'Artificial General Intelligence'. See: Fjelland, R. 'Why general artificial intelligence will not be realized,' *Humanit Soc Sci Commun* 7, 10 (2020). https://doi.org/10.1057/s41599-020-0494-4.

Data Protection

The personal data used in AI can be data that is:[242]

(1) Consciously provided by individuals, such as data given in online forms, or for particular services.

(2) Observed data that is derived from observations on individuals, for example by online tracking cookies, CCTV or devices that connect to the Internet.

(3) Derived data that is created from other data, for example the number of times an individual buys a particular item based on a retailer's sales information.

(4) Inferred data is where more complex methods of analysis are applied to find correlations between datasets and to make assessments about an individual.

Derived and inferred data are considered to be personal data in data protection law.[243] The ICO considers data that 'reveal' or 'concern' any of the special category data characteristics in UK GDPR Article 9(1) are also considered to come within the definition of personal data and this will include where the data can be inferred.[244]

The difficulty with AI for data protection is that AI models apply multiple types of data and often in large quantities. This can be problematic in relation to compliance with some of the data protection

[242] Abrams, Martin, 'The origins of personal data and its implications for governance' OECD, March 2014: http://informationaccountability.org/wp-content/uploads/Data- Origins-Abrams.pdf

[243] See EDPB approved the A29WP's 'Guidelines on the right to data portability under Regulation 2016/679'.

[244] ICO, 'What is Special Category Data': https://ico.org.uk/for-organisations/guide-to-data-protection/guide-to-the-general-data-protection-regulation-gdpr/lawful-basis-for-processing/special-category-data/.

principles, in particular the first data protection principle of lawfulness, transparency and fairness.

Lawfulness

The two lawful grounds that are most likely to be relied upon in the application of data protection to AI is UK GDPR Article 6(1)(a) 'consent' and Article 6(1)(f) 'legitimate interest'. There may also be situations where the AI is being used to provide a service to the individual, in which case Article 6(1)(b) could be relevant.

Consent

The GDPR has a strict definition of consent. It must be ***informed*** consent, such that inactivity or silence will not be valid (see Chapter IV). If any one of the elements or further caveats for consent is not met, then the controller does not have valid consent to process the data.[245] Where the organisation is processing the personal data on the basis of consent for multiple purposes, it will need consent for all of those purposes.[246] The underlying principle is that a data subject gives consent to process his or her personal data, on the understanding that they are in control of that data, and that it will be processed only for the specified purpose for which it has been given.

Where consent applies to the processing of one of the special categories of data, according to GDPR Article 9(2)(a), it must be explicit.[247] This means that the data subject must give an express statement of consent.[248] The GDPR does not prescribe how an organisation should obtain explicit

245 See the recent investigation by CNIL into Google's reliance on consent to process personal data for advert personalisation. Google was fined 50 million euros for lack of transparency, inadequate information and lack of valid consent. The EDPB press release is available here: https://edpb.europa.eu/news/national-news/2019/cnils-restricted-committee-imposes-financial-penalty-50-million-euros_en

246 See GDPR recital 32.

247 GDPR Article 9(2) outlines other exceptions, but for the majority of controllers explicit consent will be required.

248 European Data Protection Board 'Guidelines 05/2020 on consent under Regulation 2016/679', adopted 4 May 2020, paragraph 93.

consent, but the EDPB suggests that where appropriate a controller should ideally receive a written statement signed by the data subject, or some other recorded confirmation.[249] The ICO expresses a similar view.[250]

Further processing of the personal data (for the same or a different purposes) should not be based on another lawful ground other than consent once that consent is withdrawn. That is, generally, the organisation should not switch its legal basis. If consent is withdrawn, all data processing operations based on consent must stop, and the personal data must be deleted unless there is another lawful basis for continuing to hold or process the personal data. This means that where a controller needs to process personal data for multiple purposes, it must carefully assess the legal bases on which it intends to rely, before collecting the data.

As discussed in Chapter III, the lawful grounds and purpose for each processing operation must be determined at the outset.[251] If the organisation wants to continue to process personal data on another lawful basis, it cannot 'silently migrate' from consent to another lawful basis without first informing the data subject.[252] The organisation is obliged to assess whether or not it is appropriate to continue to process personal data once consent has been withdrawn.[253] The burden is on the organisation to show that it has obtained valid consent.[254]

The conditions for valid consent pose some difficulty for AI, where there may be limited human involvement in how it operates. How AI using big data would obtain accurate, specific consent – and in circumstances

[249] Ibid.

[250] See: https://ico.org.uk/for-organisations/guide-to-data-protection/key-dp-themes/guidance-for-the-use-of-personal-data-in-political-campaigning-1/special-category-data/#whatis2

[251] European Data Protection Board 'Guidelines 05/2020 on consent under Regulation 2016/679', adopted 4 May 2020, paragraphs 116 to 120.

[252] Ibid., paragraph 120.

[253] Ibid., paragraph 118.

[254] GDPR Article 7 and recital 42.

where special category data is used, explicit consent – is unclear. The ICO suggests that new technological processes could overcome this issue, for by example linking 'just in time' notification with consent processes so that an application can seek consent at the point it wants to share data with a third party.[255] The EU Agency for Network and Information Security ('ENISA') suggests the use of software agents to provide consent on the data subject's behalf.[256] It also proposes the possibility that user actions, such as a gesture or motion, could be integrated into sensors and smart devices to indicate consent.

Legitimate interests

Given the difficulties with obtaining consent to rely on it as a lawful basis, it is likely that those developing AI are likely to consider the lawful basis of legitimate interests as an alternative.

This legal basis involves a balancing exercise between the 'interests or fundamental rights and freedoms of the data subject' and the legitimate interests pursued by the organisation.[257] Recital 75 explains that 'the risk to the rights and freedoms of natural persons' will vary in likelihood and severity depending upon the context of the data processing operation. The potential negative outcomes include physical, material, or non-material damage; examples given include discrimination, identity theft, fraud and damage to reputation.[258]

The legitimate interest must be linked to the data processing operation, necessary to the processing operation and not speculative.[259] If there is another more suitable lawful basis, or less intrusive processing is possible,

---

[255] ICO guidance 'Big data, artificial intelligence, machine learning and data protection', 9 April 2017, paragraph 59.

[256] D'Acquisito, Giuseppe et al., 'Privacy by design in big data. An overview of privacy enhancing technologies in the era of big data analytics', ENISA, 17 December 2015.

[257] GDPR Article 6(1)(f).

[258] See GDPR recital 75.

[259] Article 29 Working Party 'Opinion 06/2014 on the Notion of Legitimate Interests of the Data Controller under Article 7 of Directive 95/46/EC', adopted on 9 April 2014.

then the use of legitimate interests as a basis will not be valid and the controller should consider whether another lawful ground in Article 6(1) is more suitable. The GDPR, in recitals 47 to 49, gives examples of legitimate interest as: fraud prevention, direct marketing, intra-company data transfers and network security.

The controller must also conduct a legitimate interest assessment that is relevant to the individual data subject(s). Given that the processing of personal data may have a different impact on the 'interests or fundamental rights and freedoms' of the particular data subject, a blanket approach is often not suitable. Further, the expectations of the data subject must be taken into account before relying on this ground. According to GDPR recital 47, the controller must consider '*whether a data subject can reasonably expect at the time and in the context of the collection of the personal data that processing for that purpose may take place*'.

Another problem with this lawful basis is that any subsequent processing of the personal data on this lawful ground must be compatible with the original legitimate purpose. Again, the expectations of the data subject are relevant such that if the purpose of the further processing is not closely proximate to the initial purpose, then the original lawful basis of legitimate interest may not be used. In making that decision an organisation should refer to recital 50 of the GDPR and the ICO's guidance 'Guide to the General Data Protection Regulation (GDPR) Principles – Principle (a) Lawfulness, Fairness and Transparency'.

According to GDPR recital 50 the following considerations are relevant:

- Any link between those purposes and the purposes of the intended further processing;

- the context in which the personal data have been collected, in particular the reasonable expectations of data subjects based on their relationship with the controller as to their further use;

- the nature of the personal data;

- the consequences of the intended further processing for data subjects; and
- the existence of appropriate safeguards in both the original and intended further processing operations.

The basis of legitimate interest is often problematic for organisations, in particular in adequately conducting the balancing exercise between individual's rights and their own legitimate purpose. In the context of AI, where data is collected from multiple sources, this assessment can be even more difficult because the context in which the personal data was collected may not be clear. Scraping information from the Internet, in particular social media, should be approached with a high degree of caution. As the ICO puts it, '*just because people have put data onto social media without restricting access does not necessarily legitimise all further use of it. The fact that data can be viewed by all does not mean anyone is entitled to use it for any purpose or that the person who posted it has implicitly consented to further use*'.[260]

Data Accuracy

As highlighted in some of the previous chapters of this book, data accuracy can be problematic in the use of personal data in new technologies. The ICO warns that results of data analysis in a big data, AI context is that it '*may not be representative of the population as a whole*'.[261] Moreover, even if the data analysed is recorded accurately, it cannot be assumed that the conclusions that can be made based on that analysis are accurate.[262] There is a distinction between causation and correlation and organisations using AI need to consider this in determining the accuracy of any resulting decision.[263] It is important to understand that the outputs of AI algorithms have probabilistic elements

[260] ICO guidance 'Big data, artificial intelligence, machine learning and data protection', 9 April 2017, paragraph 64.

[261] Ibid., paragraph 44.

[262] Ibid., paragraphs 93 and 94.

[263] Ibid., paragraph 118.

and are not certain.[264] The scalability of AI means that seemingly small error rates can be hugely increased.[265]

The ICO also warns of the possibility of bias and inaccuracy being fed into the AI model through the human labelling of a training dataset, in particular in relation to profiling.[266] The ICO cites some real-life examples of the types of discrimination that occurs in automated profiling. In the UK, a female doctor was locked out of the changing rooms at her gym because the automated security system had profiled her as male because the system only identified the title 'Dr' with men.[267] In the U.S., the Federal Trade Commission found evidence that credit limits were being set based on the analysis of profiles, such that a person could be deemed to have a lower credit score by being placed in a profile group with people who had poor repayment histories or shopped in the same stores.[268]

Research by the European Parliament highlights the fact that people who experience discrimination from AI systems are likely to face significant difficulties in challenging the discrimination because of the speed, scale and complexity of AI decisions and the likely reluctance of the controllers of the systems to reveal how those decisions are being made.[269]

Fairness

Fairness is one of the fundamental principles of data protection law and yet, it can be a difficult principle to understand from the point of view of a person who has 'lost out' through the application of automated profiling. For example, micro-segmentation analytics by insurers can

---

264 Office of the United Nations High Commissioner for Human Rights, 'The right to privacy in the digital age' A/HRC/48/31, 15 September 2021, paragraph 18.

265 Ibid.

266 ICO guidance 'Big data, artificial intelligence, machine learning and data protection', 9 April 2017, paragraph 96.

267 Ibid., paragraph 32.

268 Ibid., paragraph 33.

269 Tambiana Madiega and Hendrik Mildebrath, European Parliamentary Research Service, 'Regulating Facial Recognition' PE 698.021, September 2021.

more accurately gauge risk. By separating insured people into categories of risk, a person who would have been considered at high risk of being insured, could subsequently benefit from a more tailored assessment.[270] This may seem unfair to other people in the high-risk group, but overall would provide a more accurate premium level.

In data protection, fairness is related to a data subject's expectations. The question is whether a particular use of personal data would be within the reasonable expectation of the data subject. Even though the use of personal data in AI may be complex, organisations must still consider whether people could reasonably expect their personal data to be used in the ways that big data analytics facilitates.[271]

People's attitudes to the use of their personal data are often difficult to gauge and most likely vary depending on the context. A person may be unconcerned about how their personal data is used for research into how their spending decisions create demand for a particular product, but may be more likely to object if their personal data was being used in a way that discriminated or harmed other persons. For example, they may object if they found out their facial images had been scraped off the Internet to create a facial recognition tool that was then being used by some people to harass or stalk women.

Studies vary in their conclusions about public attitudes to the use of personal data:

- The Future Foundation (commissioned by the Direct Marketing Association) found that the percentage of absolute objectors to data sharing fell by 31% to 24% between 2012 and 2015.[272]

- The International Institute of Communications found that people's attitudes varied depending on a number of factors,

---

270 ICO guidance 'Big data, artificial intelligence, machine learning and data protection', 9 April 2017, paragraph 37.

271 Ibid., paragraph 29.

272 Ibid., paragraph 42.

including how much the person trusted the organisation and the type of information.[273]

- The Boston Consulting Group found that the privacy of personal data was considered a top issue for 75% of people in most countries, including younger persons.[274]

- KPMG's global survey concluded that on average, 56% of respondents were "concerned" or "extremely concerned" about how companies use their personal data.[275]

Transparency

The first data protection principle requires controllers to be transparent and fair to data subjects when processing their personal data. Transparency underpins the requirement of Articles 13 and 14 of the UK GDPR for organisations to provide data subjects with information about how and why their data is being processed ('the information requirement'). Organisations are required to communicate this information to the data subject '*in a concise, transparent, intelligible and easily accessible form, using clear and plain language*' (UK GDPR Article 12(1)). In practice, this is often achieved by providing a 'privacy' or 'information' notice.

According to UK GDPR Article 13(f) information about '*the existence of automated decision-making, including profiling, referred to in Article 22(1) and (4) and, at least in those cases, meaningful information about the logic involved, as well as the significance and the envisaged consequences of such processing for the data subject*' must also be provided.

In the context of AI, the principle of transparency will require developers of the AI product or system to inform data subjects of how their personal data is being used not only at the 'input' stage, but also to explain the

273 Ibid., paragraph 43.

274 Ibid.

275 Ibid.

'output' stage. That is, how will the AI output be used and for what purpose. For example, will it be making predictions about them (or others)? Will it be making recommendations? Will it be profiling or classifying personal data in some way or form?

In this author's view, it will also be necessary, in order to comply with the notice requirements in Articles 13 and/or 14, to explain to the data subject precisely how they are able to exercise their data subject rights (see Chapter III) in relation to the AI product, process or system. While many information notices use a generic approach when processing data in a straightforward way, the complexity of AI will most likely require more thought. This will take two aspects. First, those developing AI will need to consider how data rights can be exercised when designing the system. Second, those applying or using the AI will have to make it readily understandable to the data subject how this is practically achieved.

Purpose Limitation

The principle of purpose limitation could present a barrier to the use of personal data in AI models. Article 5(1)(b) of the UK GDPR contains the data protection principle of purpose limitation:

> Personal data shall be '*collected for specified, explicit and legitimate purposes and not further processed in a manner that is incompatible with those purposes; further processing for archiving purposes in the public interest, scientifical historical research purposes or statistical purposes shall, in accordance with article 89(1), not be considered to be incompatible with the initial purposes*'.

There is clear difficulty with this principle for AI development, where often in the early stages of development the potential application and use of the particular AI in a product or system may not be fully defined or known. The combination and reuse of datasets of personal data is what usually creates economic value and innovation and the context in which it was originally collected may be far removed from its ultimate contribution to AI.[276]

The ICO states that purpose limitation exists to prevent arbitrary re-use of personal data, but does not necessarily act as '*an insuperable barrier to extracting the value from data*'.[277] The key factor is compatibility and whether the further processing is fair.[278] Where the further processing involves using the data to detect trends or correlation, without making decisions affecting individuals, the ICO considers that the processing is likely to be compatible.[279] However, where the further processing has a purpose that affects the privacy of individuals or other fundamental rights then an organisation will need to consider '*whether it is within their reasonable expectations that their data could be used in this way*'.[280]

Where an organisation is using personal data that it has acquired, it will need to undertake due diligence to assess whether the new processing is compatible with the original purpose for which the data was collected.[281]

Future Developments

In April 2021 the European Commission proposed a regulation to harmonize the rules on AI ('EU AI Regulation').[282] A detailed exploration of the EU AI Regulation goes beyond the scope of this book, but it is likely it will be applicable to many organisations who are using and developing AI. This is because like the GDPR, the EU AI Regulation is expected to have extraterritorial effect and contain similar high penalties

---

[276] World Economic Forum 'Unlocking the Value of Personal Data: From Collection to Usage', February 2013, p.7

[277] ICO guidance 'Big data, artificial intelligence, machine learning and data protection', 9 April 2017, paragraph 78.

[278] Ibid., page 81.

[279] Ibid., paragraph 80.

[280] Ibid., paragraph 81.

[281] Ibid., paragraph 83.

[282] Proposal for a Regulation of the European Parliament and of the Council laying down harmonised rules on Artificial Intelligence (Artificial Intelligence Act), COM(2021) 206 final, 21 April 2021.

for non-compliance. It will also be the first piece of comprehensive legislation on AI globally.

The EU AI Regulation will adopt a risk-based approach to AI applications and categorises them into four groups: unacceptable risk, high risk, limited risk and minimal risk. The Commission is proposing that unacceptable risk applications are banned entirely. High risk applications will be subject to strict obligations, including human oversight measures. Limited risk applications will have specific transparency obligations, and minimal risk applications can be freely deployed. The Commission anticipates that the regulation would enter into force in the second half of 2022 and be applicable in the second half of 2024 at the earliest.

In the UK, the Government is proposing changes to data protection law to encourage innovation and the growth of the data economy. Included in its proposals are changes to the lawful basis of legitimate interest, removing the necessity of human oversight in an automated decision-making process, a new test for anonymity, changing cookie rules, and removing the necessity for a DPIA and data protection officers. The new data policy is in its early stages. As yet it is unclear how any new legislation will be able to make such profound changes to the requirements of the GDPR, while retaining the 'Adequacy' decision granted by the European Commission to allow frictionless transfers of personal data to take place between the UK and the EU.[283]

The Government's 'National AI Strategy' outlines three so-called 'pillars' to make the UK a global leader in AI innovation and development in the next decade.[284] The Government wants to increase access to data and to explore how privacy-enhancing technologies can be used to remove barriers to data sharing by managing the risks associated with sharing

[283] For more on international data transfers see my article 'Brexit and Data Protection in the UK', 27 January 2021: https://privacylawbarrister.com/2021/01/27/brexit-and-data-protection-in-the-uk/

[284] 'National AI Strategy', presented by the Secretary of State for Department for Digital, Culture, Media and Sport, September 2021: https://assets.publishing.service.gov.uk/government/uploads/system/uploads/attachment_data/file/1020402/National_AI_Strategy_-_PDF_version.pdf

commercially sensitive data and personal data. The UK government's Office for AI will publish a White Paper on regulating AI in 2022.

Useful resources on AI:

The ICO's 2018-2021 Technology Strategy.

The ICO's AI Auditing Framework.

The ICO and Turing institute's 'Project ExplAIn'.

EDPS 'Opinion 7/2015, Meeting the challenges of big data'.

CHAPTER TEN

CONCLUSION

The massive technological advances that have occurred in the past two decades have brought extraordinary benefits to economies and societies. These new technologies are using increasing amounts of personal data and as they become more advanced, will collect greater amounts of biometric data. Whether the data protection framework that exists can accommodate this phenomenon is yet to be seen. This book has described the difficulties that organisations may have in relation to ensuring compliance with the UK GDPR and DPA 2018. In particular, many of the characteristics of AI are difficult to reconcile with fundamental aspects of the data protection principles.

Many applications of AI are likely to profile individuals, or groups of individuals, to analyse behaviour. Profiling usually results in the creation of inferred or derived data from which predictions can be made about a person. This capability is useful to many organisations across all sectors, allowing them to tailor goods and services. It has benefits in the public sector too, to be able to allocate resources effectively. However, the problem is that if these predictions are inaccurate, the entire exercise fails to achieve its purpose. Bias and discrimination may also creep into models that are used to make important decisions.

While profiling to determine someone's likes and preferences in the items they choose to purchase may seem fairly innocuous, profiling to determine a person's credit worthiness, insurability, suitability for a job, or whether they qualify for access to certain services can have serious consequences. Further, although not a legal consideration, profiling has the potential to deepen inequality in society and should give us all pause for thought.

It is yet to be determined how far data protection and privacy law can be relied upon to challenge new technologies when they have negative consequential effects. While the UK GDPR places certain obligations on organisations using personal data, the burden is still on the individual data subject to challenge the organisation. The individual must first be aware of the fact that their data is being used unlawfully, or in a way to which they object. However, most of these technologies are being used on a large scale and the impact to one individual may be imperceptible, or, as in the case of the Cambridge Analytica scandal, the harm could be societal rather than impacting just one particular individual.

The challenge for Government is to create a regulatory environment that promotes and enables organisations to innovate using technology and data for the benefit of the economy and society, while ensuring fundamental rights are safeguarded. In a fast-evolving technological environment this is a difficult task, but one that will be critical.

MORE BOOKS BY
LAW BRIEF PUBLISHING

A selection of our other titles available now:-

'A Practical Guide to Transgender Law' by Robin Moira White & Nicola Newbegin
'Artificial Intelligence – The Practical Legal Issues (2nd Edition)' by John Buyers
'A Practical Guide to Challenging Sham Marriage Allegations in Immigration Law' by Priya Solanki
'A Practical Guide to New Build Conveyancing' by Paul Sams & Rebecca East
'A Practical Guide to Inherited Wealth on Divorce' by Hayley Trim
'A Practical Guide to Shareholder Disputes in Family Businesses' by Ed Weeks
'A Practical Guide to the Law of Forests in Scotland' by Philip Buchan
'A Practical Guide to Health and Medical Cases in Immigration Law' by Rebecca Chapman & Miranda Butler
'A Practical Guide to Bad Character Evidence for Criminal Practitioners by Aparna Rao
'A Practical Guide to Environmental Enforcement' by Christopher Badger & Stuart Jessop
'A Practical Guide to Hoarding and Mental Health for Housing Lawyers' by Rachel Coyle
'A Practical Guide to Psychiatric Claims in Personal Injury – 2nd Edition' by Liam Ryan
'Stephens on Contractual Indemnities' by Richard Stephens
'A Practical Guide to the EU Succession Regulation' by Richard Frimston
'A Practical Guide to Solicitor and Client Costs – 2nd Edition' by Robin Dunne
'Constructive Dismissal – Practice Pointers and Principles' by Benjimin Burgher
'A Practical Guide to Religion and Belief Discrimination Claims in the Workplace' by Kashif Ali
'A Practical Guide to the Law of Medical Treatment Decisions' by Ben Troke

'Fundamental Dishonesty and QOCS in Personal Injury Proceedings: Law and Practice' by Jake Rowley
'A Practical Guide to the Law in Relation to School Exclusions' by Charlotte Hadfield & Alice de Coverley
'A Practical Guide to Divorce for the Silver Separators' by Karin Walker
'The Right to be Forgotten – The Law and Practical Issues' by Melissa Stock
'A Practical Guide to Planning Law and Rights of Way in National Parks, the Broads and AONBs' by James Maurici QC, James Neill et al
'A Practical Guide to Election Law' by Tom Tabori
'A Practical Guide to the Law in Relation to Surrogacy' by Andrew Powell
'A Practical Guide to Claims Arising from Fatal Accidents – 2nd Edition' by James Patience
'A Practical Guide to the Ownership of Employee Inventions – From Entitlement to Compensation' by James Tumbridge & Ashley Roughton
'A Practical Guide to Asbestos Claims' by Jonathan Owen & Gareth McAloon
'A Practical Guide to Stamp Duty Land Tax in England and Northern Ireland' by Suzanne O'Hara
'A Practical Guide to the Law of Farming Partnerships' by Philip Whitcomb
'Covid-19, Homeworking and the Law – The Essential Guide to Employment and GDPR Issues' by Forbes Solicitors
'Covid-19, Force Majeure and Frustration of Contracts – The Essential Guide' by Keith Markham
'Covid-19 and Criminal Law – The Essential Guide' by Ramya Nagesh
'Covid-19 and Family Law in England and Wales – The Essential Guide' by Safda Mahmood
'A Practical Guide to the Law of Unlawful Eviction and Harassment – 2nd Edition' by Stephanie Lovegrove
'Covid-19, Residential Property, Equity Release and Enfranchisement – The Essential Guide' by Paul Sams and Louise Uphill
'Covid-19, Brexit and the Law of Commercial Leases – The Essential Guide' by Mark Shelton
'A Practical Guide to Costs in Personal Injury Claims – 2nd Edition' by Matthew Hoe

'A Practical Guide to the General Data Protection Regulation (GDPR) – 2nd Edition' by Keith Markham
'Ellis on Credit Hire – Sixth Edition' by Aidan Ellis & Tim Kevan
'A Practical Guide to Working with Litigants in Person and McKenzie Friends in Family Cases' by Stuart Barlow
'Protecting Unregistered Brands: A Practical Guide to the Law of Passing Off' by Lorna Brazell
'A Practical Guide to Secondary Liability and Joint Enterprise Post-Jogee' by Joanne Cecil & James Mehigan
'A Practical Guide to the Pre-Action RTA Claims Protocol for Personal Injury Lawyers' by Antonia Ford
'A Practical Guide to Neighbour Disputes and the Law' by Alexander Walsh
'A Practical Guide to Forfeiture of Leases' by Mark Shelton
'A Practical Guide to Coercive Control for Legal Practitioners and Victims' by Rachel Horman
'A Practical Guide to Rights Over Airspace and Subsoil' by Daniel Gatty
'Tackling Disclosure in the Criminal Courts – A Practitioner's Guide' by Narita Bahra QC & Don Ramble
'A Practical Guide to the Law of Driverless Cars – Second Edition' by Alex Glassbrook, Emma Northey & Scarlett Milligan
'A Practical Guide to TOLATA Claims' by Greg Williams
'A Practical Guide to Elderly Law – 2nd Edition' by Justin Patten
'A Practical Guide to the Law of Prescription in Scotland' by Andrew Foyle
'A Practical Guide to the Construction and Rectification of Wills and Trust Instruments' by Edward Hewitt
'A Practical Guide to the Law of Bullying and Harassment in the Workplace' by Philip Hyland
'How to Be a Freelance Solicitor: A Practical Guide to the SRA-Regulated Freelance Solicitor Model' by Paul Bennett
'A Practical Guide to Prison Injury Claims' by Malcolm Johnson
'A Practical Guide to the Small Claims Track - 2nd Edition' by Dominic Bright
'A Practical Guide to Advising Clients at the Police Station' by Colin Stephen McKeown-Beaumont

'A Practical Guide to Antisocial Behaviour Injunctions' by Iain Wightwick
'Practical Mediation: A Guide for Mediators, Advocates, Advisers, Lawyers, and Students in Civil, Commercial, Business, Property, Workplace, and Employment Cases' by Jonathan Dingle with John Sephton
'The Mini-Pupillage Workbook' by David Boyle
'A Practical Guide to Crofting Law' by Brian Inkster
'A Practical Guide to Spousal Maintenance' by Liz Cowell
'A Practical Guide to the Law of Domain Names and Cybersquatting' by Andrew Clemson
'A Practical Guide to the Law of Gender Pay Gap Reporting' by Harini Iyengar
'A Practical Guide to the Rights of Grandparents in Children Proceedings' by Stuart Barlow
'NHS Whistleblowing and the Law' by Joseph England
'Employment Law and the Gig Economy' by Nigel Mackay & Annie Powell
'A Practical Guide to Noise Induced Hearing Loss (NIHL) Claims' by Andrew Mckie, Ian Skeate, Gareth McAloon
'An Introduction to Beauty Negligence Claims – A Practical Guide for the Personal Injury Practitioner' by Greg Almond
'Intercompany Agreements for Transfer Pricing Compliance' by Paul Sutton
'Zen and the Art of Mediation' by Martin Plowman
'A Practical Guide to the SRA Principles, Individual and Law Firm Codes of Conduct 2019 – What Every Law Firm Needs to Know' by Paul Bennett
'A Practical Guide to Adoption for Family Lawyers' by Graham Pegg
'A Practical Guide to Industrial Disease Claims' by Andrew Mckie & Ian Skeate
'A Practical Guide to Redundancy' by Philip Hyland
'A Practical Guide to Vicarious Liability' by Mariel Irvine
'A Practical Guide to Applications for Landlord's Consent and Variation of Leases' by Mark Shelton
'A Practical Guide to Relief from Sanctions Post-Mitchell and Denton' by Peter Causton
'A Practical Guide to Equity Release for Advisors' by Paul Sams
'A Practical Guide to Financial Services Claims' by Chris Hegarty

'The Law of Houses in Multiple Occupation: A Practical Guide to HMO Proceedings' by Julian Hunt
'Occupiers, Highways and Defective Premises Claims: A Practical Guide Post-Jackson – 2nd Edition' by Andrew Mckie
'A Practical Guide to Financial Ombudsman Service Claims' by Adam Temple & Robert Scrivenor
'A Practical Guide to Advising Schools on Employment Law' by Jonathan Holden
'A Practical Guide to Running Housing Disrepair and Cavity Wall Claims: 2nd Edition' by Andrew Mckie & Ian Skeate
'A Practical Guide to Holiday Sickness Claims – 2nd Edition' by Andrew Mckie & Ian Skeate
'Arguments and Tactics for Personal Injury and Clinical Negligence Claims' by Dorian Williams
'A Practical Guide to Drone Law' by Rufus Ballaster, Andrew Firman, Eleanor Clot
'A Practical Guide to Compliance for Personal Injury Firms Working With Claims Management Companies' by Paul Bennett
'RTA Allegations of Fraud in a Post-Jackson Era: The Handbook – 2nd Edition' by Andrew Mckie
'RTA Personal Injury Claims: A Practical Guide Post-Jackson' by Andrew Mckie
'On Experts: CPR35 for Lawyers and Experts' by David Boyle
'An Introduction to Personal Injury Law' by David Boyle
'A Practical Guide to Subtle Brain Injury Claims' by Pankaj Madan

These books and more are available to order online direct from the publisher at www.lawbriefpublishing.com, where you can also read free sample chapters. For any queries, contact us on 0844 587 2383 or mail@lawbriefpublishing.com.

Our books are also usually in stock at www.amazon.co.uk with free next day delivery for Prime members, and at good legal bookshops such as Wildy & Sons.

We are regularly launching new books in our series of practical day-to-day practitioners' guides. Visit our website and join our free newsletter to be kept informed and to receive special offers, free chapters, etc.

You can also follow us on Twitter at www.twitter.com/lawbriefpub.

www.ingramcontent.com/pod-product-compliance
Ingram Content Group UK Ltd.
Pitfield, Milton Keynes, MK11 3LW, UK
UKHW020147290926
15471UKWH00004B/739

9 781913 715939